CLERGYMEN
OF THE
CHURCH OF
ENGLAND

CLERGYMEN OF THE CHURCH OF ENGLAND

Anthony Trollope

With an introduction by

Michael Mayne

DARTON · LONGMAN + TODD

Published in 2010 by
Darton, Longman and Todd Ltd
1 Spencer Court
140 – 142 Wandsworth High Street
London
SW18 4JJ

First published in 1866 by Chapman & Hall,
reprinted from the *Pall Mall Gazette*

Introduction © Michael Mayne
Illustrations © David Eccles

ISBN 978-0-232-52846-6

Printed and bound in Great Britain
by Page Bros, Norwich, Norfolk

CONTENTS

INTRODUCTION

In March, 1993, as Dean of Westminster, I dedicated
a memorial to Anthony Trollope in a window in
Poets' Corner. Not before time. The *Athens News*,
reporting the event with a misprint that might have
delighted him, referred to me as "the bear of
Westminster". Trollope, no expert on bears, knew
something of the Abbey and was a connoisseur of
deans. Two years before writing these essays he
had petitioned for a memorial to Thackeray in Poets'
Corner, and nine years earlier (in *The Warden*) he
describes how Mr Harding, with a day to fill in
London, attends morning service in the Abbey.

Mr Harding was not much edified by the nature
of the service. The minor canon in question
hurried in, somewhat late, in a surplice not in
the neatest order, and was followed by a dozen
choristers, who were also not as trim as they
might have been: they all jostled into their
places with a quick hurried step, and the service
was soon commenced. Soon commenced and

soon over – for there was no music, and time
was not unnecessarily lost in the chanting. On
the whole, Mr Harding was of the opinion that
things were managed better at Barchester,
though even there he knew there was room for
improvement.[1]

As for deans: only one who has been a dean
himself "can distinctly define the duties of a Dean of
the Church of England", which would appear merely
"to reside and show himself, and the city which he
graces by his presence will hardly demand of him
other services"; though it is of course understood
that the dean, though "always sleeker than a
bishop", will nevertheless "desire to become a
bishop, though he would lose by the change of his
easy comfort, his sufficient modest home, and the
grace of his close in which no one overtops him".[2]
Dean Alford of Canterbury was so touched on the
raw that, in an extensive attack, he attacked
Trollope's ignorance of the clergy and accused him
of having a "hair-dresser's estimate of mankind".[3]

When these essays first appeared in the *Pall Mall
Gazette* a few months before Trollope embarked on
The Last Chronicle of Barset, the Church of
England – like the British Army – was organised on
a system that was obsolete and furnished with
equally obsolete equipment. Fortunately the British
Army did not have to meet the Germans: the Church
of England was less fortunate, and did. In the shape
of Biblical Criticism originating in Germany. Until
the 1860s most Englishmen assumed the Bible to be

true as history, even if the more educated were doubting the exact accuracy of the early parts of Genesis. (Darwin's *Origin of Species* appeared in 1859.) The German scholars began to study each book of the Bible as an ancient historical document that needed to be put into a social context. In 1860 two Anglican clergymen, Jowett of Balliol and Frederick Temple (later Archbishop of Canterbury), considering there to be an unhealthy reticence over the study of the Bible, published *Essays and Reviews*. It was a solid attempt to come to terms with new theological issues and by the turn of the century its alleged heresies were to become commonplaces. Yet it was roundly condemned by Convocation (though acquitted by the courts), and eleven thousand clergymen signed a petition of faithfulness to the strictest doctrine of the verbal inerrancy of scripture and to the literal accuracy of the Genesis account of creation. At this mid-point of Victoria's reign, it must have been hard for a man or woman of any intellectual calibre to retain their faith in the form in which it was almost universally proclaimed from Anglican pulpits; and the fact that the Evangelicals, still in 1860 the strongest group of churchmen in England, had become timid and Tory, and that the Anglo-Catholics, a brilliantly reforming force under Newman, Keble and Pusey a quarter of a century earlier, had no acquaintance with scientific theology, made it hard for such as Matthew Arnold (though he remained a shadowy Christian believer) not to hear the Sea of Faith's "melancholy, long, withdrawing roar, Retreating..." in 'Dover

Beach'[4]. The voices of intelligent agnostics had begun to be heard.

Liberal theological and scriptural views were popularised through the work of such men as Bishop Colenso of Natal. A distinguished mathematician – though no great scholar – he had read *Essays and Reviews* and decided to produce a study of the first five books of the Old Testament, the Pentateuch. He worked out (and hastily rejected) that six men had 2,748 sons and each priest would have been compelled to eat 88 pigeons daily. In 1863 Bishop Gray of Cape Town took him to court on a charge of heresy and he was found guilty and deprived of his bishopric. He appealed to the Privy Council which judged him still legally to be Bishop of Natal. Bishop Gray thereupon excommunicated him. Colenso refused to step down and remained legally Bishop of Natal until his death. The evangelical J.C. Ryle, later Bishop of Liverpool, believed in the inspired truth of every word of the Old Testament to the end of his life, and in a preface to a book attacking Colenso (entitled *Moses, or the Zulu?*) he wrote: "If the Bishop of Natal is let alone ... the Church of England will be disgraced in the eyes of Christendom, as a church whose Bishops went to the stake for truth in the sixteenth century, but tolerated undisguised infidelity within her pale in 1863..."[5]

It was a time, then, of serious intellectual questioning and of doubt – considered by the Evangelicals to be synonymous with temptation. A time too, of an antiquated church, its clergy underpaid, its laity much preached-at but largely uninformed, its bishops tending to withdraw defensively at the first sign of critical Biblical scholarship. And, if we are to believe Matthew Arnold, the one topic of public interest on which you could be "certain of having a crowded meeting in any large town in England" in almost any decade of the nineteenth century, was not Darwinism or the Corn Laws or Biblical scholarship, but the question of the Disestablishment of the Church of England.[6] Yet what is of such interest to the church historian is that through all the times of turmoil and passion following the Reformation, through the Civil War and Commonwealth, through the sluggish worldliness of the eighteenth-century church and the missionary expansion and conservatism of the Victorian age, the English parson is the focus and pivot of the Church's history. And in the Anglican tradition, while he is also both priest and preacher, he is chiefly *pastor*, his work classically defined in the life and writings of George Herbert, his unchanging role in the English parish system – whatever his churchmanship – that of the care and cure of souls.

Trollope knew this. This is why he describes "the parish parson" (as opposed in his day to "the town incumbent") as "pure parson and nothing else", the one who "must know that he has got himself into that place for which he has been expressly fitted by the orders he has taken", the one who "throughout his whole life has lived in close communion with rural affairs, and has of them that exact knowledge which close communion only will give".[7] But Trollope was a Church of England man to his finger -tips: brought up in an Anglican home, educated at an Anglican school, he admitted that when he got his postal clerkship he knew nothing of arithmetic but could name every bishop in the Church of England.[8] "For myself," he wrote, "I love the name of State and Church, and believe that much of our English well-being has depended on it." And George Eliot wrote of him: "(He) is a Church of England man, clinging to whatever is, *on the whole*, and without fine distinctions, honest, lovely and of good report".[9] Attracted to the simple certainty of Irish Catholicism, he nevertheless deemed it not to be a religion for "gentlemen".[10] He was drawn rather to that other continuity of style that runs like a watermark through English post-Reformation history, what one might call the defining marks of Anglicanism: tolerance within a broad spectrum of belief and interpretation; a high regard for the individual conscience; moderation in face of extremism; a recognition that sometimes the truth may lie in both extremes rather than somewhere in between. He was attracted to the growing theological liberalism of his time in face of a rigid, stubbornly unchanging orthodoxy. He welcomed the "creeping doubts" that had become common among Anglicans by the end of his life.

Not that such Anglican qualities as moderation and tolerance prevented him from having robustly critical views about the all-invasive Evangelicals. The Trollopes and their circle found the

Evangelicals ("for many years past ... in the ascendant"[11]), with their moralising, their great emphasis on preaching at the expense of the sacraments, and their frequent fundamentalist views, tiresome; Anthony's brother Tom thought that Evangelicalism was "the sort of thing that might be expected to be met with in tradesmen's back parlours ... but was utterly out of place among gentlemen..."[12], a view both brothers absorbed from their mother, who in her novels blasted both Evangelicals and Catholics alike. Few of Trollope's Evangelical clergy are sympathetic, although in *Rachel Ray* Samuel Prong is an exception, being a "devout, good man; not self-indulgent ... sincere, hard-working, sufficiently intelligent, true in most things to the instincts of his calling". Yet not perfect, for he is "deficient in the one vital qualification for a clergyman of the Church of England; he was not a gentleman".[13]

In October 1863 the *Christian Remembrancer* struck a despairing note: "It will very soon indeed cease to be taken as a matter of course that a clergyman is a gentleman... We can scarcely doubt but that an observer retaining in his remembrance what the clerical order as a body is now, if the system of "literates" continues, will in fifty years' time look back to the gentlemanly dignified clergy of his youth, *refined even in their errors* (my italics); and contrast them with the ruder manners and rougher vices of the time he lives in." And, as a parting shot, the writer adds: "A socialist English clergy is no remote possibility".[14] It has been said that for Trollope the gentleman is a moral ideal, and his essays on the Modern English Archbishop, the Bishop, the Archdeacon and the Parish Parson are shot through with references to the social class which it is assumed to be the background of all clergy worth their salt. "The man who won't drink his glass of wine, and talk of his college, and put off for a few happy hours the sacred stiffnesses of the profession and become simply an English gentleman, – he is the clergymen whom in his heart the archdeacon does not love".[15] That same archdeacon who "is necessarily – I may say certainly – a gentleman. Alas! that the day should have gone by when the same might have been said of every clergyman bearing orders in the Church of England".[16] But no longer can it be assumed that all clergy are products of Oxbridge, for "there are the theological colleges here and there, and men and women talk of "literates..." Yet Trollope does not doubt that the result will be "an altered man, and as a man less attractive, less urbane, less genial, – in one significant word, less of a gentleman..." And in every country parish the rustic will "take his new parson between his finger and thumb and find out whether he be a gentleman ... (for) the gentleman he will obey and respect, in the gentleman he will believe".[17]

While the gentlemanly English country parson may be Trollope's ideal, much was wrong with the system that had until all too recently allowed a sometimes scandalous use of patronage and plurality, and which kept many curates in

considerable penury. Two laymen, Lord Liverpool
and Sir Robert Peel, had sought to put the house in
order: Lord Liverpool, Prime Minister from 1812 to
1827, beginning to make a proper use of patronage,
in which Sir Robert Peel conscientiously followed
him. Peel, moreover, created the Ecclesiastical
Commission in 1835, which was the start of the
administrative reformation of the Church of
England. Until that time the Church's organisation
and abuses were still medieval and quite
unreformed. But clergy pay remained low, in the
case of curates a disgrace. Few thanked Trollope for
pointing it out. When the Essays were published, the
Church paper, *The Guardian*, attacked him for his
comments on their low income: it was "unworthy of
Mr Trollope" to "endorse a popular error".[18] Peel
was a great reformer, but his brother-in-law had a
cathedral prebendary's stall worth £1500 a year and
four livings: a total income of £3000, out of which he
had to find some £70 a year to pay each of his four
parish curates. Trollope paints a vivid picture of the
impoverished curate, for whom at first it is a glory
"to eat bread without butter and to drink tea without
milk", but once his "religious ecstacy" deserts him –
and especially if he takes a wife – "gradually there
creeps upon him the heart-breaking disappointment
of a soured and an injured man". Trollope cares
passionately about such clear injustice – yet cannot
refrain from ending: "For men of a lower class in life,
who have come from harder antecedents, the
normal seventy pounds per annum may suffice; but
all modern Churchmen will understand what must

be the effect on the Church if such be the recruits to which the Church must trust".[19]

A few essentials have not changed: the Church of England is still established, its parish system still guarding the right to pastoral care to all who wish for it, the parish clergy, though decimated in numbers since Victorian times, still the backbone of a church of linked word and sacrament; much better paid, sometimes stretched to the limits, and no less diversely and proudly Anglican. The Reformation settlement was a comprehension, not a compromise, and there is a world of difference between them. There will always rightly be within the Church of England Catholics and Evangelicals and Liberals. At any one time one school of thought will predominate. Once again the Evangelicals are much in the ascendant, but much changed. Theologically, despite some remains of a bleak and noisy fundamentalism, the Biblical Criticism/Darwinian war is won, or rather it has shifted into new territory. The work of scientists with their "how?" questions and of theologians with their "why?" questions is understood to be complementary not opposed, and there are a sufficient number of eminent scientists who are Christians to show that science and religion are partners in their exploration of the mystery of the universe and the meaning of life.

Yet Trollope would find the world to which the church seeks to minister changed beyond belief. Two world wars, the Holocaust, the social and economic transformation of society, urbanisation, higher education, the gender revolution and an obsession with all things sexual, the break-down of conventional ethics and new ethical dilemmas have all in their different ways led to a rejection of the more subtle fundamentalism of "the Church (or the Bible) says"; it is very low tide indeed on Dover Beach, and the challenge now in England is how to interpret the reality of the God who is both creator and Christlike to a society largely ignorant of the Bible and unaware of mainstream Christian belief. And one in which most media reporting of the Church's affairs is hostile, even derisory.

Nor are today's clergy almost exclusively the products of Oxbridge. Drawn from the widest social background, a "gentleman" only in Newman's sense, perhaps, as "one who never inflicts pain",[20] many are juggling some half-dozen country parishes in their care; others are trained as non-stipendiaries or perhaps "ordained local ministers", the latter continuing to work in secular jobs serving their own community with no thought of moving elsewhere (but not because like Trollope's "curate in a populous parish" they are trapped on a pittance with no hope of advancement). No bishop, dean or archdeacon enjoys a sinecure. No town, and few country, clergy find the space for that (sometimes eccentric) expertise – ornithology, geology, writing – that gave us a Gilbert White, a Dean Buckland, a Kilvert and a George Herbert. Dioceses have multiplied. Synodical government has, negatively, brought both a vast, unwelcome growth of administration and, positively, given to clergy and laity alike a proper authority in the governance of the church. The cathedrals have a choral tradition of which they are fiercely proud, one that would have Mr Harding spinning with delight. New liturgies have understandably proved divisive but they have restored a liturgical shape and a doctrinal balance, particularly to the eucharist, that had been lost since the earliest centuries. This has been matched by the shift of emphasis from the word (Matins and Evensong) to the sacrament (the Parish Communion) that in the past seventy years has profoundly affected all traditions in the Church of England. Most thoughtful and informed Anglicans would acknowledge certain losses (the language of Cranmer and the King James' version would figure large), but significant gains.

It was whilst wandering round the Close in Salisbury on a midsummer evening in 1852 that Trollope conceived the story of *The Warden*, and while the model for Barchester is Winchester, it was this city to which I have retired that inspired that series of novels with their bishops, deans, archdeacons and assorted clergy dancing to the music of time. If he was to visit the Close at Salisbury today he would find that the greatest change of all is that the present Dean's wife is a priest. That, I think, would have struck even that great master of words momentarily speechless.

MICHAEL MAYNE
Dean Emeritus of Westminster

1   The Warden. Penguin Classics 144
2   Clergymen of the Church of England.
    Leicester University Press 1974. 33–4
3   Henry Alford. The Contemporary Review June 1866
4   Matthew Arnold. Dover Beach. 11, 25–6
5   Moses, or Zulu? A Detailed Reply to the Objections contained
    in Parts 1 and 2 of Bishop Colenso's work by the Revd. W.
    Wickes. London 1863. Preface by the revd. J.C. Ryle
6   Matthew Arnold. Last Essays on Church and Religion. 1877
7   Trollope. Ibid. 57, 60 – 1
8   Richard Mullen. Anthony Trollope. Duckworth 1990. 250
9   Ibid 251. The George Eliot Letters. New Haven 1954–78. 4.
    81–2
10 Victoria Glendinning, Trollope. Hutchinson 1992. 479
11 Trollope, 26
12 Mullen, 24
13 Mullen, 257
14 The Christian Remembrancer, October 1863, vol xlvi, 395
15 Trollope, 48
16 Trollope, 52
17 Trollope, 59–60
18 Guardian, 6 June, 1866
19 Trollope, 101–2, 104.
20 John Henry Newman, The Idea of a University: Knowledge
    and Religious Duty. Longmans, Green 1947, 185

CLERGYMEN

OF THE

CHURCH OF ENGLAND.

I.

THE MODERN ENGLISH ARCHBISHOP.

THE old English archbishop was always a prince in
the old times, but the English archbishop is a prince
no longer in these latter days. He is still a nobleman
of the highest rank,—he of Canterbury holding his
degree, indeed, above all his peers in Parliament, not
of Royal blood, and he of York following his elder
brother, with none between them but the temporary
occupant of the woolsack. He is still one before
whose greatness small clerical aspirants veil their
eyes, and whose blessing in the minds of pious
maidens has in it something almost divine. He is,

as I have said, a peer of Parliament. Above all things, he should be a gentleman, and,—if it were always possible,—a gentleman of birth ; but he has no longer anything of the position or of the attributes of a prince.

And this change has come upon our archbishops quite in latter times; though, of course, we must look back to the old days of Papal supremacy in England for the prince archbishop of the highest class. Such careers as those of Thomas à Becket or of Wolsey have not been possible to any clergymen since the days in which the power of the Pope was held to be higher on matters ecclesiastical than the power of the Crown in these realms ; but we have had among us prince archbishops to a very late date,— archbishops who have been princes not by means of political strength or even by the force of sacerdotal independence, but who have enjoyed their principalities simply as the results of their high rank, their wealth, their reserve, their inaccessibility, as the result of a certain mystery as to the nature of their duties,—and sometimes as the result of personal veneration. For this personal veneration personal dignity was as much needed as piety, and was much more necessary than high mental power. An arch-bishop of fifty years since was very difficult to approach, but when approached was as urbane as a king,—who is supposed never to be severe but at a distance. He lived almost royally, and his palace received that respect which seems, from the nature of the word, to be due to a palatial residence. What he did, no man but his own right-hand chaplain knew with accuracy; but that he could shower church patronage as from the east the west and the south, all clerical aspirants felt,—with awe rather than with hope. Lambeth in those days was not overshadowed by the opposite glories of Westminster. He of York, too, was a Northern prince, whose hospitalities north of the Humber were more in repute than those of earls and barons. Fifty years since the archbishops were indeed princes; but now-a-days we have changed all that. The change, however, is only now com-pleted. It was but the other day that there died an Archbishop of Armagh who was prince to the backbone, princely in his wealth and princely in his use of it, princely in his mode of life, princely in

his gait and outer looks and personal demeanour,—
princely also in the performance of his work. He
made no speeches from platforms. He wrote no
books. He was never common among men. He
was a fine old man ; and we may say of him that
he was the last of the prince archbishops.

This change has been brought about, partly by
the altered position of men in reference to each other,
partly also by the altered circumstances of the archbishops themselves. We in our English life are
daily approaching nearer to that republican level
which is equally averse to high summits and to
low depths. We no longer wish to have princes
among us, and will at any rate have none of that
mysterious kind which is half divine and half hocus-
pocus. Such terrestrial gods as we worship we choose
to look full in the face. We must hear their voices
and be satisfied that they have approved themselves
as gods by other wisdom than that which lies in the
wig. That there is a tendency to evil in this as well
as a tendency to good may be true enough. To be
able to venerate is a high quality, and it is coming to
that with us, that we do not now venerate much. In

this way the altered minds of men have altered the position of the archbishops of the Church of England.

But the altered circumstances of the sees themselves have perhaps done as much as the altered tendencies of men's minds. It is not simply that the incomes received by the present archbishops are much less than the incomes of their predecessors,— though that alone would have done much,—but the incomes are of a nature much less prone to produce princes. The territorial grandeur is gone. The archbishops and bishops of to-day, with the exception of, I believe, but two veterans on the bench, receive their allotted stipends as do the clerks in the Customhouse. There is no longer left with them any vestige of the power of the freehold magnate over the soil. They no longer have tenant and audit days. They cannot run their lives against leases, take up fines on renewals, stretch their arms as possessors over wide fields, or cut down woods and put acres of oaks into their ecclesiastical pockets. They who understand the nature of the life of our English magnates, whether noble or not noble, will be aware of the worth of that territorial position of which our bishops have been deprived under the working of the Ecclesiastical Commission. The very loss of the risk has been much!—as that man looms larger to himself, and therefore to others also, whose receipts may range from two to six hundred a year, than does the comfortable possessor of the insured medium. The actual diminution of income, too, has done much, and this has been accompanied by so great a rise in the price of all princely luxuries that an archbishop without a vast private fortune can no longer live as princes should live. In these days, when a plain footman demands his fifty pounds of yearly wages, and three hundred pounds a year is but a moderate rent for a London house, an archbishop cannot support a semi-royal retinue or live with much palatial splendour in the metropolis upon an annual income of eight thousand pounds.

And then, above all, the archbishops have laid aside their wigs.

That we shall never have another prince archbishop in England or in Ireland may be taken to be almost certain. Whether or no we shall ever have prelates at Canterbury or York, at Armagh or Dublin, gifted with the virtues and vices of princely minds, endowed with the strength and at the same time with the self-willed obstinacy of princes, may be doubtful. There is scope enough for such strength and such obstinacy in the position, and our deficiency or our security,—as each of us according to his own idiosyncrasy may regard it,—must depend, as it has latterly been caused, by the selections made by the Prime Minister of the day. There is the scope for strength and obstinacy now almost as fully as there was in the days of Thomas à Becket, though the effects of such strength or obstinacy would of course be much less wide. And, indeed, as an archbishop may be supposed in these days to be secure from murder, his scope may be said to be the fuller. What may not an archbishop say, and what may not an archbishop do, and that without fear of the only punishment which could possibly reach an archbishop,—the punishment, namely, of deprivation? With what caution must not a Minister of the present day be armed to save him from the misfortune of having placed an archbishop militant over the Church of England?

The independence of an archbishop, and indeed to a very great, though lesser extent of a bishop, in the midst of the existing dependence of all others around him, would be a singular phenomenon, were it not the natural result of our English abhorrence of change. We hate an evil, and we hate a change. Hating the evil most, we make the change, but we make it as small as possible. Hence it is that our Archbishop of Canterbury has so much of that independent power which made Thomas à Becket fly against his sovereign when the archiepiscopal mitre was placed upon his head, though he had been that sovereign's most obedient servant till his consecration. Thomas à Becket held his office independently of the king; and so does Dr. Longley. The Queen, though she be the head of the Church, cannot rid herself of an archbishop who displeases her. The Queen, in speaking of whom in our present sense of course we mean the Prime Minister, can make an Archbishop of Canterbury; but she cannot unmake him. The archbishop would be safe, let him play what tricks he might in his high office. Nothing short of a commission de lunatico inquirendo could attack

him successfully,—which, should it find his grace to
be insane, would leave him his temporalities and his
titles, and simply place his duties in the hands of a
coadjutor. Should an archbishop commit a murder,
or bigamy, or pick a pocket, he, no doubt, would be
liable to the laws of his country; but no lawyer and
no statesman can say to what penalties he can be
subjected as regards the due performance of the
duties of his office. A judge is independent;—that
is, he is not subject to any penalty in regard to any
exercise of his judicial authority; but we all know
that a judge would soon cease to be a judge who
should play pranks upon the bench, or decline to
perform the duties of his position. The archbishops,
as the heads of the endowed clergymen of the Church
of England, are possessed of freeholds, and that freehold cannot be touched. It is theirs for life; and so
great is the practical latitude of our Church, that it
may be doubted whether anything short of a professed
obedience to the Pope could deprive an archbishop of
his stipend.

It may, therefore, be easily understood that a
Prime Minister, in selecting an archbishop, has a

difficult task in hand. He is bound to appoint a man who not only has hitherto played no pranks, but of whom he may feel sure that he will play none in future. In our Church, as it exists at present, we have ample latitude joined to much bigotry, and it is almost as impossible to control the one as the other. Such control is, in fact, on either side absolutely impossible; and, therefore, archbishops are wanted who shall make no attempts at controlling. And yet an archbishop must seem to control,—or, else, why is he there? An Archbishop of Canterbury must be a visible head of bishops, and yet exercise no head-ship. He must appear to men as the great guide of parsons, but his guidance must not go beyond advice, and of that the more chary he may be, the better will be the archbishop. Of course it will be understood that reference is here made to doctrinal guidance, and not to moral guidance—to latitude or bigotry in matters of religion, and not to the social conduct of clergymen. How difficult then must be the position of a Minister who has to select for so dangerous a place a clergyman who shall be great enough to fill it, and yet small enough; and one who shall also be just enough to remember always that he is bound to retain that quiescence for which credit was given him when he was chosen? The archbishop must be a man without any latent flame, without ambition, desirous of no noise, who shall be content to have been an archbishop without leaving behind him a peculiar name among his brethren. He should hope to be remembered only as a good old man, who in troublesome times abated some trouble and caused none, who smiled often and frowned but seldom, who wore his ecclesiastical robes on high days with a grace, and exercised a modest and frequent hospitality, having no undue desire to amass money for his children.

It is not, perhaps, too much to say that the sort of man exactly wanted may be selected for any post, and be found adequate to the required duties so long as the sword of deprivation or dismissal can be made to hang over the occupant's head. But it is very difficult to find a man who shall do his work, not after the fashion which may seem best to himself, but in the way which seems most desirable to others, who, when once placed, cannot be removed from his

place. Will your groom or your gardener obey you
with that precision which you desire when he comes
to know that you cannot rid yourself of his services ?
And human nature is the same in gardeners and
in archbishops. It is not that the man is void of
conscience and that he resolves to disobey where he
has promised to obey, but that he tells himself that
in his position duty requires no obedience. Your
gardener with a taste for tulips would, under such
circumstances, grow nothing but tulips ; and what is
to hinder your archbishop from putting down the
miracles or putting up candlesticks ? With Lambeth
all ablaze with candlesticks the archbishop would still
hold his place.

The same thing may be said of the bishops ; but
among so many bishops it is felt to be well that there
should be some few who shall have a flame of their
own. In the house that has many rooms the owner
may indulge in many colours on the walls, and some
of them may be of the brightest ; but in the house
that has but one or two chambers the colours should
be chosen with a due regard to the ordinary quiescence
of every-day life. Had we not High Church and Low

The Modern English Archbishop.
"Nothing should shock him——"

Church among our ordinary bishops, were we to be deprived of our dear —— and our dear ——, we should miss much that we feel to be ornamental to the Establishment and useful to ourselves. There are a few among us of course who would be glad to see lights of the same splendour, even though so dangerous, at Canterbury and at York; but it behoves a Prime Minister to be a moderate man, and a man moderate, above all things, in religion. In the religion of to-day moderation is everything. And, therefore, whatever else he may be, let the archbishop be a moderate man. Let him always be throwing oil upon waters. Nothing should shock him—nothing, that is, in the way of religion. Nothing should excite him; nothing should make him angry. He should be a man able to preach well, but not inclined to preach often. In his preaching he should charm the ears of all hearers, but he should hardly venture to stir their pulses. He should speak, too, occasionally from platforms and chairs; only let him not make himself too common. He should be very affable on Mondays and Tuesdays, secluding himself somewhat on the other five days of the week, answering his correspondents with words which may mean as little as words can be made to mean, and carefully watching that he commits himself to nothing. How hard it is to find the man who shall have talent enough for this, and yet the self-command never to go beyond it, even though no penalties await him, except such as may come from the venomous baiting of other clergymen.

But it must not be supposed that the archbishop of to-day can be, or should be, an idle man. It is his duty to be the precursor—probably the unconscious precursor—of other men in that religion which shall teach us that the ways of God are very easy to find, though they may not be so easy to follow; that forms are almost nothing, so that faith be there. Of all men, an archbishop should be the least of a fanatic. Can any one imagine an archbishop of the present day abhorring a Dissenter, or refusing to dine with a Roman Catholic because of his religion? And to do this is much, even though it be done unconsciously. An archbishop thus leading the van against bigotry has to stand with placid unmoved front against assailants by the hundred. Let us only think of the letters that are addressed to him, of the attacks made upon him, of the questions asked of him. Against every attack he must defend himself, and yet must he never commit himself. He must never be dumb, and yet must he never speak out boldly. He must be always true to the Thirty-nine Articles, and yet never fight for any one of them. In the broad his creed must be infallible, but he himself may make a standing-point on no detail. To carry an archbishop's mitre successfully under such circumstances requires much diligence, considerable skill, imperturbable good humour, and undying patience.

The selections that have been made by the Ministers of the Crown for the last twenty or twenty-five years have all apparently been made on the principle of selecting such archbishops as have been here described, and English Churchmen in general seem to think that the Ministers of the Crown have exercised wise discretion in the appointments which they have made.

II.

ENGLISH BISHOPS, OLD AND NEW.

IF it were said that the difference between bishops of the old school and of the new consists chiefly in the fact that the former wore wigs and that the latter have ceased to do so, the definition would be true enough if it were followed out, not literally, but with a liberal construction. In former days the wig and apron, of themselves, almost sufficed ; but now, these outer things having been, to so great an extent, laid aside, other things, much more difficult of acquirement, are needed. There was, however, such an odour of pious decorum round the episcopal wig, that we cannot but regret its departure; and then, again, so much of awe has gone, now that the wig is abandoned ! We who can remember the bishops in their full panoply can hardly understand how a bishop of these times can be a bishop at all to his subject parsons. And that veneration which arose from outer circumstances used to be so peculiarly the perquisite of the bench of bishops, that men of the laity, thinking over it all, are at a loss to conceive why appendages so valuable should have been abandoned thus recklessly. Even aprons are not worn as aprons were worn of yore,— but in a shorn degree, showing too plainly that the reverend wearer is half ashamed of the tranquil decoration; and lawn sleeves themselves do not seem to envelop the occupant in so extensive a cloud of sacred millinery as they did in the more reverent days of George the Fourth. Have the bishops themselves made this suicidal change; or have they only succumbed to the invincible force of public opinion in thus abandoning those awful symbols which were so valuable to them ?

A full and true answer to this question would go far towards giving a history of the Church of England during the last sixty or seventy years,— from the days in which Lord Eldon was first consulted as to the making of a bishop, down to the last decade of years in which bishops are popularly supposed to have been selected in accordance with the advice of a religious Whig nobleman. Such a history cannot be given here, but the peculiarities of the old and new bishop may perhaps be so described as to show something of the result of the changes that have taken place.

The bishop of George the Third and George the Fourth was never a prince, as was the archbishop,— but he was a wealthy ecclesiastical baron, having the prestige of a Peer of Parliament, even when he did not use the power, living like a great lord in his palace, drawing his income from territorial domains, —an income which was often so much greater than his needs as to afford him the means of amassing a colossal fortune. And as he generally entered upon the possession of this income without any of the encumbrances which are incidental to the hereditary possessors of great properties, and usually considered himself to be precluded by the nature of his profession from many of those wealth-consuming pursuits to which his lay brother nobles are prone, it came to pass that the bishop was ordinarily a rich man. He kept no race-horses; he was not usually a gambler; he could provide for clerical sons and clerical sons-in-law out of the diocesan pocket: and was preserved by the necessary quiescence of clerical life from that broadcast magnificence which is so costly to our great nobles, because it admits of no check upon its expenditure. The bishop, let him live as handsomely as he might, was not called upon to live beyond the scope of accounts;—and many of our bishops were good accountants.

But in those halcyon days, there was this drawback to being a bishop, that the good things did not all come at once. What was a bishopric with three thousand a year, when there were others of equal rank with seven, or eight, or occasionally with ten thousand,—not to speak of the sublimity of Canterbury, or the magnificence of York, or the golden opulence of Durham, or the ancient splendour of Winchester, or the metropolitan glory of London? The interest which made a bishop could translate a bishop, and, therefore, no bishop in those days could rest in comfortable content in the comparatively poor houses of Exeter or Gloucester, while Ely might be reached, or at least Worcester. Thus it came to pass that men, who in those days were never young when they were first chosen, were still living always in hope of some rich change; and that when the rich change came at last, the few remaining years, the wished-for opportunities of wealth, were used with a tenacity of purpose which might almost put a usurer to the blush.

But it would be unreasonable to feel strong abhorrence against the old bishops on this account. Men in all walks of life do as others do around them, and bishops are but men. It was thought to be the proper thing that a bishop should exercise his power over the domains of the see to the utmost extent rendered possible by the existing law. He would run his life against a lease on the ecclesiastical property. If he died before the lease expired the benefit would be to his successor. If he survived he could lease the property for a term of years to his son at a peppercorn rent, and the see would be so far robbed. It was an interesting, exciting mode of life, and as the ecclesiastical lands grew in value as all lands grew,—town lands, for instance, which gradually covered themselves with houses,—the game became so delightful that it is almost a pity that it should have been brought to an end. Let no man say to himself that had he been a bishop in those days he would have done otherwise,— unless he is quite sure that he is better than those around him, even in these days.

But when such good things were going who were the men who got them? And to this may be added a further question, How far did they deserve the good things which were given to them? It used to be said that there were three classes of aspirants to bishoprics, and three ladders by which successful clergymen might place themselves on the bench. There was the editor of the Greek play, whose ladder was generally an acquaintance with Greek punctuation. There was the tutor of a noble pupil, whose ladder was the political bias of his patron. And there was he who could charm the royal ear, whose ladder was as frequently used in the closet as in the pulpit. To these was afterwards added the political aspirant,— the clergyman who could write a pamphlet or advocate a semi-ecclesiastical cause by his spoken or written words.

That scholarship should be remunerated was very well; that men in power should reward those who had been faithful to themselves and their children was, at any rate, very natural; that the Sovereign should occasionally have a voice in making those selections which, as head of the Church, it was popularly supposed that he always made, seemed only to be fair;—and who can say that a Minister was wrong to recompense ecclesiastical support by ecclesiastical preferment? But it must be admitted that the bench of bishops as it was constituted under the circumstances above described was not conspicuous for its clerical energy, for its theological attainments, or for its impartial use of the great church patronage which it possessed. They who sat upon it ordinarily wore their wigs with decorum and lived the lives of gentlemen; but, looking back for many years, a churchman of the Church of England cannot boast of the clerical doings of its bishops. Under the great wig system much of awe was engendered, and that amount of good was attained which consists mainly of respect and reverence for the unknown. The mere existence of a Llama is good for people

who have no more clearly expressed God to worship,
—and in this way the old, rich, bewigged bishops
were serviceable. But, with a few exceptions, they
did but little other clerical service. New churches
were not built under their auspices, nor were old
churches repaired. Dissent in England became
strong, and the services of the State Church were in
many dioceses performed with a laxity and want even
of decency which, though it existed so short a time
since, now hardly obtains belief. The wigs have
gone, but in their places have come,—as we are
bound to acknowledge,—many of those qualities,
much more difficult of acquirement, which men
demand when wigs will no longer satisfy them. Let
any middle-aged man of the present day think of
the bishops of his youth, and remember those who
were known to him by report, repute, or perhaps by
personal intercourse. Although bishops in those
days were not common in the market-places as they
are now, some of us were allowed to see them and
hear them speak, and most of us may have some
memory of their characters. There were the old
bishops who never stirred out, and the young bishops

who went to Court ; and the bishop who was known to be a Crœsus, and the bishop who had so lived that, in spite of his almost princely income, he was obliged to fly his creditors ; and there was the more innocent bishop who played chess, and the bishop who still hankered after Greek plays, and the kindly old bishop who delighted to make punch in moderate proportions for young people, and a very wicked bishop or two, whose sins shall not be specially designated. Such are the bishops we remember, together with one or two of simple energetic piety. But who remembers bishops of those days who really did the work to which they were set ? In how many dioceses was there a Boanerges of whom the Church can be proud ? It is almost miraculous that the Church should have stood at all through such guidance as it has had.

This has now been much altered, and the modern bishop is at any rate a working man. And while we congratulate ourselves on the change that has been made, let us give thanks where thanks are due. No doubt the increased industry of the bishops has come, as has the increased industry of public officers, from the demand of the people whom they are called upon to serve. But in no way and by no means has more been done to create this energy than by that movement at Oxford which had its beginning hardly more than thirty years since, and of which the two first leaders are still alive. Dr. Newman has gone to Rome, and Dr. Pusey has perhaps helped to send many thither; but these men, and their brethren of the Tracts, stirred up throughout the country so strong a feeling of religion, gave rise by their works to so much thought on a matter which had been allowed for years to go on almost without any thought, that it may be said of them that they made episcopal idleness impossible, and clerical idleness rare. Of course, it will be said, in opposition to this, that no school of clergymen has so run after wiggeries and vestments and empty symbols as have the followers of the men whom I have named. But the wiggeries and vestments have been simply the dross which has come from their fused gold. If you will make water really boil, some will commonly boil over. They have built new churches, and cleansed old churches, and opened closed churches.

They have put on fuel and poked the fire, till heat does really issue from it. It is not only with the High Church,—with their own brethren,—that they have prevailed, but equally with the Low Church, whose handsome edifices and improved services are due to that energy which has been so hateful to them.

The modern bishop is a working man, and he is selected in order that he may work. He is generally one who has been conspicuous as a working parish clergyman, and may be and often is as ignorant of Greek as his former parish clerk. In discussing archbishops it has been said that the chosen candidate must have no strong Church predilections of his own. In choosing a bishop a Minister is bound by no such limit. Perhaps it would be well if High Church, Low Church, and Broad Church could be allowed to have their turns in rotation,—as used to be the case with the two universities. For many years past the Low Church has been in the ascendant, and the chances now are that in meeting a bishop one meets an enemy of the Oxford movement. But the bishop's own predilections matter little, perhaps,

English Bishops, Old and New
"——— *sitting in cabs...*"

if the man will work with a will.   There are few,
I think, now who remember much of the Low Church
peculiarities of the Bishop of London, having for-
gotten all that in the results of his episcopate.

But, alas, in losing our fainéant bishops we have
lost the great priest lords whom we used to venerate.
A bishop now has no domain, but is paid his simple
salary of 5,000*l.* a year,—quarterly, we suppose,—
and knows not and recks not of leases.   He is
paid 5,000*l.* a year if his see was in former days
worth as much, or less if the see of old was worth
less.   London, Durham, and Winchester are more
gorgeous than their brethren, but even London and
Durham have simple salaries, and Winchester, on
the next vacancy, will be reduced to the same
humble footing.   It is a great fall in worldly state,
and consequently bishops may be now seen,—as
bishops never were seen of yore,—sitting in cabs,
trusting themselves to open one-horse chaises,
talking in the market-places, and walking home
after an ordination.   These ears have heard and
these eyes have seen a modern bishop hallooing
from the top of his provincial High-street to a groom

who was at the bottom of it, brandishing his episcopal arms the while with an energy which might have been spared. It is so with all things. In seeking for the useful, we are compelled to abandon the picturesque. Our lanes and hedgerows and green commons are all going; and the graceful dignity of the old bishop is a thing of the past.

There still, however, remains to the bench one privilege, which, though shorn of its ancient grandeur of injustice, has in it still much of the sweet mediæval flavour of old English corruption. The patronage of the bishops is as extensive almost as ever; and though its exercise is now hemmed in by certain new stringencies of ecclesiastical law,—as in regard to pluralities, and is also subject to the scrutiny of public opinion, so that decency must at least be respected,—nevertheless patronage remains, as the private property of the bishop. A bishop is not bound, even in theory as the theory at present exists, to bestow his patronage as may be best for the diocese over which he presides. He still gives, and is supposed to give, his best livings to his own friends. A deserving curate has no claim on a bishop for a living as a reward for the work he has done. The peculiarly strong case of a Mr. Cheese may, here and there, give rise to comment; but unless the nepotism is too glaring, nepotism in bishops is allowed ;—nay, it is expected. A bishop's daughter is supposed to offer one of the fairest steps to promotion which the Church of England affords.

Is it not singular that it should be so,—that the idea of giving the fitting reward to the most deserving servant should have to reach the Church the last of all professions and of all trades ? Sinecures and the promotion of young favourites used to be common in the Civil Service ; but the public would not endure it, and the Civil Service has cleansed itself. The army and navy have been subjected to searching reforms. A great law officer has been made to vanish into space because he was too keen in appropriating patronage to family uses. Bankers and brewers will no longer have men about their premises who do not work; and yet bankers and brewers may do what they like with their own. But the bishop, in whose hands patronage has been placed, that he might use it in the holiest way for the highest purpose, still

exercises it daily with the undeniable and acknowledged view of benefiting private friends! And in
doing so he does not even know that he is doing
amiss. It may be doubted whether the bishop has
yet breathed beneath an apron who has doubted that
his patronage was as much his own as the silver
in his breeches-pocket. The bishop's feeling in the
matter is not singular, but it is singular that bishops
should not before this have been enlightened on the
subject of Church patronage by the voice of the laity
whom they serve.

III.

THE NORMAL DEAN OF THE PRESENT DAY.

IF there be any man, who is not or has not been a Dean himself, who can distinctly define the duties of a Dean of the Church of England, he must be one who has studied ecclesiastical subjects very deeply. When cathedral services were kept up for the honour of God rather than for the welfare of the worshippers, with an understanding faintly felt by the indifferent, but strongly realized by the pious, that recompence would be given by the Almighty for the honour done to Him,—as cathedrals were originally built and adorned with that object,—it was natural enough that there should be placed at the head of those who served in the choir a high dignitary who, by the weight of his presence and the grace of his rank, should give an increased flavour of ecclesiastical excellence to those services. The dean then was the head, as it were, of a college, and he fitly did his work if he looked after the ceremonies of his cathedral, saw that canons, precentor, minor canons and choristers, did their ministrations with creditable grace, took care that the building was, if possible, kept in good repair,—and thus properly took the lead in the chapter over which he presided. But the idea of honouring our Creator by the excellence of our church services, — though it remains firmly fixed enough in the minds of some of us,—is no longer a national idea; and we may say that deans are not selected by those who have the appointment of deans with any such view. We use our cathedrals in these days as big churches, in which multitudes may worship, so that, if possible, they may learn to live Christian lives. They are made beautiful that this worship may be attractive to men, and not for the glory of God. What architect would now think it necessary to spend time and money in the adornment of parts of his edifice which no mortal eye can reach ? But such was done in the old days when deans were

The Normal Dean of the Present Day
"architectural ecclesiastics..."

first instituted.   Multitudes, no doubt, crowded
our cathedrals in those times, — when bishops and
deans were subject to the Pope—but they were
there for the honour of God, testifying their faith by
the fact of their presence.   That all this has been
changed need hardly be explained here; but in the
change it would seem that the real work of the dean
has gone,—except so far as it may please him to take
some part in those offices of the church service which
it is necessary that a clergyman should perform.   It
is now ordinarily believed that to the dean is especially entrusted the care of the structure itself; and
luckily for us, who love our old cathedrals, we have
had some deans of late who, as architectural ecclesiastics, have been very serviceable; but should a
dean have no such tendencies,—as many deans have
had none,—no penalty for neglect of prescribed duty
would fall upon him.   A certain amount of yearly
residence is enjoined; and it is expected, of course,
that a dean should show himself in his own cathedral.   Let him reside and show himself, and the
city which he graces by his presence will hardly
demand from him other services.

In truth, the lines of deans have fallen in pleasant places. Man, being by nature restless and ambitious, desires to rise; and the dean will desire to become a bishop, though he would lose by the change his easy comfort, his sufficient modest home, and the grace of his close in which no one overtops him. To be a Peer of Parliament, to rule the clergy of a diocese, and wear the highest order of clerical vestment, is sweet to the clerical aspirant. A man feels that he is shelved when he ceases to sing excelsior to himself in his closet. But the change from a deanery of the present day to a palace is a change from ease to work, from leisure to turmoil, from peace to war, from books which are ever good-humoured to men who are too often ill-humoured. The dean's modest thousand a year sounds small in comparison with the bishop's more generous stipend:—but look at a dean, and you will always see that he is sleeker than a bishop. The dean to whom fortune has given a quaint old house with pleasant garden in a quaint old close, with resident prebendaries and minor canons around him who just acknowledge, and no more than acknowledge, his superiority,—who takes the lead, as Mr. Dean, in the society of his clerical city,—who is never called upon to discharge expensive duties in London, though he may revisit the glimpses of the metropolitan moon for a month, perhaps, in the early summer, showing his new rosette at his club,—seems indeed to have had his lines given to him in very pleasant places.

There is something charming to the English ear in the name of the Dean and Chapter. None of us quite know what it means, and yet we love it. When we visit our ancient cathedrals, and are taken into a handsome but manifestly useless octagonal stone outhouse, we are delighted to find that the chapter-house is being repaired at an expense of, say, four thousand pounds, subscribed by the maiden ladies of the diocese; or if we find the said outhouse to be in ruins,—in which case the afflicted verger will not show it if we allow him to pass easily through our hands,—we feel a keen regret as though all things good were going from us. That there should be a chapter-house attached to the cathedral, simply because a chapter-house was needed in former days, is all the reason that we can give for our affection; and we think that the old ladies have spent their money

well in preserving the relic. We also think that the
Ecclesiastical Commission spends its money well in
preserving the chapter, and should feel infinite regret
in finding that any diocese had none belonging to it.
We are often told that ours is a utilitarian age, but
this utilitarian spirit is so closely mingled with a
veneration for things old and beautiful from age that
we love our old follies infinitely better than our new
virtues.

Though it is difficult to define the duties of a
modern dean, we all of us know what are the qualities
and what the acquirements which lead to deaneries in
these days; and most of us respect them. As it is
now necessary that a man shall have been an active
parish parson before he is thought fit to be a bishop,
so it is required that a clergyman shall have shown a
taste for literature in some one of its branches before
he can be regarded among the candidates proper for
a deanery. The normal dean of this age is a gentleman who would probably not have taken orders
unless the circumstances of his life had placed orders
very clearly in his path. He is not a man who has
been urged strongly in early youth by a vocation for

clerical duties, or who has subsequently devoted himself to what may be called clerical administrations
proper. He has taken kindly to literature, having
been biassed in his choice of the branch which he has
assumed by the fact of the word " Reverend " which
has attached itself to his name. He has done well
at the university, and has been a fellow, and perhaps
a tutor, of his college. He has written a book or
two, and has not impossibly shown himself to be too
liberal for the bench; for it is given to deans to speak
their thoughts more openly than bishops are allowed
to do. Indeed, this is so well acknowledged a principle in the arrangement of church patronage, that it
has struck many of us with wonder that the Government has not escaped from its difficulty in regard
to the Bishop of Natal by making him a dean in
England.

And, when once a dean, the happy beneficed lover
of letters need make no change in the mode of his
life, as a bishop must do. He is not driven to feel
that now and from henceforth he must have his neck
in a collar to which he has hitherto been unused, and
that he must be drawing ever and always against the

hill. A bishop must do so, or else he is a bad bishop; but a dean has got no hill before him, unless he makes one for himself.

Who that knows any of our dear old closes,—that of Winchester, for instance, or of Norwich, or Hereford, or Salisbury,—has not wandered among the modest, comfortable clerical residences which they contain, envying the lot of those to whom such good things have been given? The half-sequestered nook has a double delight, because it is only half sequestered. On one side there is an arched gate,—a gate that may possibly be capable of being locked, which gives to the spot a sweet savour of monastic privacy and ecclesiastical reserve; while on the other side the close opens itself freely to the city by paths leading, probably, under the dear old towers of the cathedral, by the graves of those who have been thought worthy of a resting-place so near the shrine. It opens itself freely to the city, and courts the steps of church matrons, who are almost as clerical as their lords. It is true, indeed, that much of their glory has now departed from these hallowed places. The dean still keeps his deanery, but the number of resident canons has been terribly diminished. Houses intended for church dignitaries are let to prosperous tallow-chandlers, and in the window of a mansion in a close can, at this moment in which I am writing, be seen a notice that lodgings can be had there by a private gentleman—with a reference. But still it is the Close. There is still an odour there to the acutely percipient nostrils as of shovel hats and black vestments. You still talk gently as you walk over its well-kept gravel, and would refrain within its precincts from that strength of language which may perhaps be common to you out in the crowded marts of the city. The cathedral, at any rate, is there, more beautiful than ever,—thanks to the old ladies and the architectural dean. The musical rooks fly above your head. The tower bells delight your ear with those deep-tolling, silence-producing sounds which seem to come from past ages in which men were not so hurried as they are now; and you feel that the resident tallow-chandler and the single gentleman with a reference have not as yet destroyed the ancient piety of the place.

The dean and chapter! How pleasantly the

words sound on the tongue of a reverent verger! The chapters, I fear, are terribly shorn of their old glory, and each chapter must look at itself, when it meets, with something of wistful woe in its half-extinguished old eyes. And why does a chapter meet? Its highest duty is a congé d'élire,—permission to choose its own bishop. Permission is sent down from the Prime Minister to the chapter to choose Dr. Smith,—a very worthy evangelical gentleman, whose name stinks in the nostrils of the old high and dry canons and prebendaries who still hang round the towers of the cathedral; and, — under certain terrible penalties,—they exercise their functions, and unanimously elect Dr. Smith as the bishop of that diocese. There must be something melancholy in such moments to a reflective dean and chapter. We may suppose that the number of clerical gentlemen who really meet together to carry on the business of the election is not great. It is as small, probably, as may be; but something of a chapter must be held. The ignorant layman, as he thinks of it, wonders whether the work is really done in that cold unfurnished octagonal stone building, which has just been so beautifully repaired at the expense of the devout maiden ladies.

How English, how absurd, how picturesque it all is!—and, we may add, how traditionally useful! The Queen is the head of the Church, and therefore sends down word to a chapter, which in truth as a chapter no longer exists, that it has permission to choose its bishop, the bishop having been already appointed by the Prime Minister, who is the nominee of the House of Commons! The chapter makes its choice accordingly, and the whole thing goes on as though the machine were kept in motion by forces as obedient to reason and the laws of nature as those operating on a steam engine. We are often led to express our dismay, and sometimes our scorn, at the ignorance shown by foreigners as to our institutions; but when we ourselves consider their complications and irrationalistic modes of procedure, the wonder is that any one not to the manner born should be able to fathom aught of their significance.

Deans and chapters, though they exist with a mutilated grandeur, for the present are safe; and long may they remain so!

IV.

THE ARCHDEACON.

A DEAN has been described as a Church dignitary who, as regards his position in the Church, has little to do and a good deal to get. An archdeacon, on the other hand, is a Church dignitary, who in diocesan dignity is indeed almost equal to a dean, and in diocesan power is much superior to a dean, but who has a great deal to do and very little to get. Indeed, as to that matter of getting, the archdeacon,—as archdeacon,—may be said to get almost nothing. It is quite in keeping with the traditional polity and well understood peculiarities of our Church that much work should be required from those officers to whom no payment is allotted, or payment that is next to none; whereas from those to whom affluence is given little labour is required. And the system works well enough. There has as yet been no dearth of archdeacons; nor shall we probably experience any such calamity.

Nevertheless, archdeacons are seldom allowed to starve. The bishops have it in their power to look to that, and knówing that in these days starving men seldom can exercise much authority, they take care that their archdeacons shall be beneficed. The archdeacon always holds a living. In former happy days he not unfrequently held more than one, and there are probably archdeacons still living in that halcyon condition. He always holds a living, and almost always a good living. He not unfrequently is a man of private means, and has been selected for his position partly on that account. He is the nominee of the bishop, and is, therefore, not unfrequently intimately connected with episcopal things. He is, perhaps, the son or nephew of a bishop, or has married a wife from the palace, or has, after some fashion, sat in his early days at episcopal feet. He is one whom the bishop thinks that he can love and trust; and therefore, before he has obtained his

archdeaconry, he has probably been endowed with
that first requisite for a good servant—good wages.
A poor archdeacon, an archdeacon who did not keep
a curate or two, an archdeacon who could not give a
dinner and put a special bottle of wine upon the
table, an archdeacon who did not keep a carriage, or
at least a one-horse chaise, an archdeacon without a
man servant, or a banker's account, would be no-
where,—if I may so speak,—in an English diocese.
Such a one could not hold up his head among
churchwardens, or inquire as to church repairs with
any touch of proper authority. Therefore, though
the archdeacon is not paid for his services as archdeacon, he is generally a gentleman who is well to do
in the world, and who can take a comfortable place in
the county society among which it is his happy lot
to live.

But, above all things, an archdeacon should be a
man of the world. He should know well, not only
how many shillings there are in a pound, but how
many shillings also there are in a clerical pound,—
for in these matters there is a difference. Five
hundred a year is much more in the hands of a

country parson than it is in the hands of a country
gentleman who is not a parson,—all which the
efficient archdeacon understands and has at his fingers'
ends to the last shilling of the calculation. He
should understand, too, after what fashion his brother
rectors and vicars live around him,—should know
something of their habits, something also of their
means, and should have an eye open to their welfare,
their pursuits, and their amusements. Of all these
things the really stirring archdeacon does in fact
know very much.

The archdeacon is, in fact, a bishop in little, and
as such is often much more of a bishop in fact than
is the bishop himself. To define,—or rather to
make intelligible by any definition,—an archdeacon's
power and duties, would be very difficult; as also it
is very difficult, or I may say impossible, to do so
with reference to a bishop's functions. The archdeacon holds a court, and makes visitations. These
visitations may be made pretty much at his pleasure.
He must, I believe, make them once in three years,
but may make them every year if he thinks fit. He
inquires as to the administration of the services,

seeing that the canons are maintained, but has no power to alter aught ; and as there seems to be much difficulty in knowing when and by what the canons are maintained, and when and by what they are not maintained, we may imagine that the inquiries of a discreet archdeacon into the practices of a respectable and efficient parson will not be too close or searching in this matter of the canons. It is, however, easier to see whether the windows of a church are in repair, and whether the roof keeps out the rain, than it is to be intelligibly and efficiently explicit on the subject of canons, and, therefore, the outward structure of the parish church gives very safe employment to an archdeacon. The little difficulty as to church rates which sometimes follows upon an order for repairs is not uncongenial to the archdeacon's mind. It hinges upon politics, and upon a vexed political question in which the archdeacon, as a strong local Conservative, has hitherto had his victories. There remain so very few subjects which are still grateful to him in the same way, that church rates, with all their little impediments and embargoes, naturally present them-selves to him as pleasant matters. And then the

archdeacons receive reports from the churchwardens,
if churchwardens have anything to report,—any
scandal of which to tell, or evil practices on the
parson's side of which complaint has unfortunately
become necessary according to the judgment of those
churchwardens ! By the word " scandal " let not the
uninitiated reader be led to think that undignified
tittle-tattle with his neighbour's churchwardens is
the duty or the employment of an archdeacon. Open
moral misconduct in a clergyman's life is supposed
to be matter of justifiable public scandal—the scandal
arising with the clerical sinner, and not with those
who tell of the sin—and, as such, is, by the constitu-
tion of our Church, an especial subject for the care
of our archdeacons, and indeed, under them, of our
churchwardens. But in such matters archdeacons
are liberal, and much prefer to wink an eye than to
see too much. We may imagine that a church-
warden, misunderstanding his mission with regard to
scandal, and taking upon himself too promptly the
duty of watching the moral conduct of his parson,
would not receive much comfort from a visiting archdeacon. No one knows better than an archdeacon—

no one knows so well as an archdeacon—that it is needless and absurd to look for a St. Paul in every parsonage. He would, indeed, be very little at his own ease with a local St. Paul, much preferring a comfortable rector, who can take his glass of wine after dinner and talk pleasantly of old college days. St. Pauls, however, do not trouble him; nor is he troubled much by the scandals of his clerical neighbours; but he must be troubled sorely, I should think, by the increasing number and increasing influence around him of those "literate" clergymen who—from want of better, as we must in sorrow confess,—are flocking to us from Islington, Birkenhead, and such like fountains of pastoral care. The man who won't drink his glass of wine, and talk of his college, and put off for a few happy hours the sacred stiffnesses of the profession and become simply an English gentleman,—he is the clergyman whom in his heart the archdeacon does not love.

Thus the archdeacon is a bishop in little as regards his own archdeaconry, which may probably comprise half a diocese; and as an energetic financial secretary at the Treasury may, under an uninstructed

The Archdeacon

"...very little at his own ease with
a local St. Paul..."

Chancellor of the Exchequer, have much more to do
with the finances of the country than the Chancellor
of the Exchequer himself, so may an energetic archdeacon have a much stronger influence on his clerical
district than the bishop who is over him. He is the
bishop's eye, or should be so, and may not improbably
become the bishop's hand.

But the archdeacon, in spite of all his power and
authority, though he be so great among his brother
parsons, is hardly in the way to better promotion.
High promotion in the Church now comes from
political influence or from the friendship of Ministers,
—from those things, combined of course with high
clerical attainments—and an archdeacon is not often
in the way to obtain political influence or the friendship of Ministers. As deans live in towns, so do
archdeacons live in the country; and like other
country gentlemen they are always in opposition.
And then they are men who have been made what
they are by the bishops, and, therefore, are known
well in their dioceses, but are not much known
beyond them. They culminate in their own local
dignity, and, knowing that they do so, they make

the most of it.   An archdeacon who is potent with his bishop, and who is popular with his clergymen, who works hard and can do so without undue meddling, who has a pleasant parish of his own and is not troubled by ambitious or indifferent curates, who can live on good terms with the squires around him, understanding how far it is expedient that he should be restricted by his coat, and how far he may go in discarding hyper-clerical constraint, is master of a position in which he need not envy the success of any professional gentleman in the kingdom.   But he is not on the direct road to higher things, and will probably die in his rectory, an archdeacon to the last.

If an archdeacon be ambitious of moving in higher clerical matters than his archdeaconry affords him, he generally looks to gratify that desire by sitting in Convocation.   This method of doing something more than routine duty is easier and less likely to fail than the other method of publishing a volume of sermons. Sermons are not read now as they were some thirty or forty years since, and Convocation has lately held its head a little up, obtaining recognition in the newspapers, and appearing to do something. An archdeacon is just the man to believe that Convocation can do much; and this faith on his part is evidence of a moral freshness and a real earnestness which adds a charm to his normal character. Who can bring himself to believe that a bishop believes in Convocation—a bishop, that is, who takes his seat in the House of Lords, talks to other peers, and knows what is going on in the well-instructed blasé London world? Such a one cannot but see, cannot but know, that Convocation is a clerical toy, a mere debating society to which belongs none of the vitality of power. But the archdeacon, fresh from the country, believes in Convocation, and works there with some real conviction that he is one of a clerical Parliament, and that he is animated by true parliamentary life.

But it is in his own rectory that an archdeacon must ever shine with the brightest light. I have said that he is a bishop in little, and I may also say that he is the very chief among parsons; and as the country parson—the country parson with pleasant parsonage, pleasanter wife, and plenty of children— is the true and proper type of an English clergyman,

to which bishops, deans, canons, and curates are
mere adjuncts and necessary excrescences, so is the
archdeacon the highest type of the country parson.
He is always married—an exception here or there
would but prove the rule—he generally has a large
family; of course he has a pleasant rectory. He
must be an earnest working parish clergyman, or he
would hardly have been selected as an archdeacon.
He is necessarily—I may say certainly—a gentleman.
Alas! that the day should have gone by when the
same might have been said of every clergyman bearing orders in the Church of England. He is a man
of the world, as I have above explained, and as such
it is not probable that he will be a fanatic, though
living examples may probably be adduced that fanati-
cism can exist under an archdeacon's hat. And he
walks just a head taller than other clergymen around
him, receiving that pleasant attitude from the modest
authority which he carries. Of all attitudes it is the
most pleasant. He who stands high on a column
can hardly talk pleasantly with those who stand
round his pedestal; and that haranguing with loud
voice from column top to column top is but a cold

ceremonial conversation. Who can imagine two archbishops slapping each other's backs and being jolly together ? But an archdeacon is not raised by his dignity above a capability for jovial intimacy, and yet he walks with his head pleasantly raised above the heads of other parsons around him.

V.

THE PARSON OF THE PARISH.

THE word parson is generally supposed to be a slang
term for the rector, vicar, or incumbent of a parish,
and, in the present day, is not often used without
some intended touch of drollery,—unless by the rustics
of country parishes who still cling to the old word.
But the rustics are in the right, for of all terms by
which clergymen of the Church of England are known,
there is none more honourable in its origin than that
of parson. By that word the parish clergyman is
designated as the palpable and visible personage of
the church of his parish, making that by his presence
an intelligible reality which, without him, would be
but an invisible idea. Parsons were so called before
rectors or vicars were known, and in ages which had
heard nothing of that abominable word incumbent.
A parson proper, indeed, was above a vicar,—who

originally was simply the curate of an impersonal parson, and acted as priest in a parish as to which some abbey or chapter stood in the position of parson. The title of rector itself is new-fangled in comparison with that of parson, and has no special ecclesiastical significance. The parson, properly so called, had not only the full charge of his parish, but the full benefit derivable from the tithes ; and then he came to change his name and to be called politely a rector. The vicar was he who had the full charge of his parish, as also he has at present, vicariously at first for some abbey or chapter ; and now, in these days, vicariously for some lay impropriator, — but who had and has the benefit only of the so-called small tithes ; and then he also came to be called the parson. Rectors and vicars at present hold their livings by tenures which are equally firm, and they have done so now for more than four hundred years. The rustics above mentioned would be much surprised if told that their vicar was not a real parson. In speaking, therefore, of the parson of the parish, let us be understood to mean the parish clergyman, who has that full fruition of his living which is given by freehold possession.

There is a pleasant flavour of old crusted port present to the palate of one's imagination when mention is made of a rector, which he misses perhaps in inquiring after the vicar, whose beer may be better than his wine; and the rector cuts lustily from the haunch, while the vicar is scientific with the shoulder. But we expect, on the other hand, and are gratified in expecting, a kinder and more genial flow of clerical wit from the vicar than the rector gives us; and I have generally found the vicar's armchair to be easier than that of his elder brother. But here, in speaking of the English parson,—of the priest who has full clerical command in his parish,—no distinction between rector and vicar shall be made.

The parson of the parish is the proper type and most becoming form of the English clergyman as the captain of his ship is of the English naval officer. Admirals of the Red and Admirals of the Blue, and Commodores with authority ashore, are very fine fellows, and may perhaps be greater in their way than the captain can be in his; but for real naval efficiency and authority the captain of the ship on his own quarter-deck stands unequalled. And so it is with the parson of the parish in his own glebe. He is pure parson and nothing else, and in the daily work of his life, if he does that daily work diligently, he cannot but feel that he is devoting himself to those duties which properly belong to him. Whether a bishop in the House of Lords may so think of himself, or a bishop speaking from a platform, or a bishop in the turmoils of correspondence, or even a bishop dispensing his patronage, may be more doubtful. And the easy dean may doubt whether such ease was intended for him when he took upon himself to bear the arms of St. Paul. And the fellow of a college, even though he be tutor as well as fellow, may feel some qualms as to that word reverend with which he has caused the world to address him. But the parson in his parish must know that he has got himself into that place for which he has been expressly fitted by the orders he has taken. The curate, who is always a curate, to whom it is never given to exercise by his own right the highest clerical authority in his parish, cannot be said to have fulfilled the mission of his profession satisfactorily, let him have worked ever so nobly. He is as the lieutenant

who never rises to be a captain. But the parson
requires no further exaltation for clerical excellence.
The higher he rises above parsondom, the less will
he be of a clergyman. He may become a peer of
Parliament, or the head of a chapter, or a local magis-
trate over other clergymen, as is an archdeacon; but
as simply parish parson, he fills the most clerical
office in his profession.

The parson of the parish in England, a few years
since, was almost necessarily a man who had been
educated at Oxford or Cambridge. An English
parish might indeed have an Irishman from Trinity
College, Dublin; and, now and again, an outsider
was admitted into the fold as a shepherd. There
was a small college in the north to fit northern candidates for northern congregations, and the rule was
not absolutely absolute; but it prevailed so far that
it was felt to be a rule. And thence came an assur-
ance, in which trust was put more or less by all
classes, that the parson of the parish was at least a
gentleman. He was a man who had lived on equal
terms with the highest of the land in point of birth,
and hence arose a feeling that was very general in

rural parishes, and as salutary as it was general, that
the occupant of the parsonage was as good a man as
the occupant of the squire's house. It would be
interesting to us to trace when this feeling first
became common, knowing as we do know that for
many years after the Reformation, and down even
to a comparatively late date, the rural clergyman
was anything but highly esteemed. We are told
constantly that the parson left the dining-room when
the pudding came in, and that he by no means did
badly for himself in marrying the lady's maid. We
most of us know the character of that eminent divine
Dr. Tusher, who lived in the reign of Queen Anne.
Then came the halcyon days of British clergymen,—
the happy days of George III. and George IV., and
the parson in his parsonage was as good a gentleman
as any squire in his mansion or nobleman in his
castle. There is, alas! a new order of things coming
on us which threatens us with some changes, not for
the better, in this respect. There are theological
colleges here and there, and men and women talk
of "literates." Who shall dare to say that it may
not all be for the best? Who will venture to pro-

phesy that there shall be less energetic teaching of
God's word under the new order of things than under
the old? But, as to the special man of whom we
speak now, the English parish parson, with whom we
all love to be on familiar terms,—that he will be an
altered man, and as a man less attractive, less urbane,
less genial,—in one significant word, less of a gentleman,—that such will be the result of theological
colleges and the institution of "literates," no one
who has thought of the subject will have any doubt.

And in no capacity is a gentleman more required
or more quickly recognized than in that of a parson.
Who has not seen a thrifty household mistress
holding almost unconsciously between her finger
and thumb a piece of silk or linen, and telling at
once by the touch whether the fabric be good? This
is done with almost an instinct in the matter, and
habit has made perfect in the woman that which was
born with her. Exactly in the same way, only much
more unconsciously, will the English rustic take his
new parson between his finger and thumb and find out
whether he be a gentleman. The rustic cannot tell by
what law he judges, but he knows the article, and the

gentleman he will obey and respect, in the gentleman he will believe. Such is his nature. While in the other, who has not responded favourably to the touch of the rustic's finger, the rustic will not believe, nor by him will he be restrained, if restraint be necessary. The rustic in this may show, perhaps, both his ignorance and servility, as well as the skilled power of his fingering,—but such is his nature.

But the adult parson of the parish in England,— the clergyman who has reached, if I may so say, the full dominion of his quarter-deck,—is still customarily a man from Oxford or from Cambridge, and it is of such a one that we speak here. He has probably been the younger son of a squire, or else his father has been a parson, as he is himself. Throughout his whole life he has lived in close communion with rural affairs, and has of them that exact knowledge which close communion only will give. He knows accurately, from lessons which he has learned unknowingly, the extent of the evil and the extent of the good which exists around him, and he adapts himself to the one and to the other. Against gross profligacy and loud sin he can inveigh boldly, and he

can make men and women to shake in their shoes
by telling them of the punishment which will follow
such courses; but with the peccadilloes dear to the
rustic mind he knows how to make compromises, and
can put up with a little drunkenness, with occasional
sabbath-breaking, with ordinary oaths, and with
church somnolence. He does not expect much of
poor human nature, and is thankful for moderate
results. He is generally a man imbued with strong
prejudice, thinking ill of all countries and all
religions but his own; but in spite of his prejudices
he is liberal, and though he thinks ill of men, he
would not punish them for the ill that he thinks.
He has something of bigotry in his heart, and would
probably be willing, if the times served his purpose,
to make all men members of the Church of England
by Act of Parliament; but though he is a bigot, he
is not a fanatic, and as long as men will belong to his
Church, he is quite willing that the obligations of
that Church shall sit lightly upon them. He loves
his religion and wages an honest fight with the devil;
but even with the devil he likes to deal courteously,
and is not averse to some occasional truces. He is

quite in earnest, but he dislikes zeal; and of all men whom he hates, the over-pious young curate, who will never allow ginger to be hot in the mouth, is the man whom he hates the most. He carries out his Bible teaching in preferring the publican to the Pharisee, and can deal much more comfortably with an occasional backslider than he can with any man who always walks, or appears to walk, in the straight course.

It almost seems that something approaching to hypocrisy were a necessary component part of the character of the English parish parson, and yet he is a man always on the alert to be honest. It is his misfortune that he must preach higher than his own practice, and that he is driven to pretend to think that a stricter course of life is necessary than that which he would desire to see followed out even in his own family. As the mealman in the description of his flours can never go below "middlings," knowing that they who wish to get the cheapest article would never buy it if it were actually ticketed as being of the worst quality, so is the parson driven to ticket all his articles above their real value. He cannot tell his people what amount of religion will

really suffice for them, knowing that he will never get
from them all that he asks ; and thus he is compelled
to have an inner life and an outer,—an inner life, in
which he squares his religious views with his real
ideas as to that which God requires from his
creatures; and an outer life, in which he is always
demanding much in order that he may get little.
From this it results that a parish parson among his
own friends differs much from the parish parson among
his parishioners, and that he is always, as it were,
winking at those who know him as a man, while he
is most eager in his exercitations among those who
only know him as a clergyman.

The parish parson generally has a grievance, and
is much attached to it,—in which he is like all other
men in all other walks of life.   He not uncommonly
maintains a mild opposition to his bishop, upon
whom he is apt to look down as belonging to a new
order of things, and whom he regards, on account of
this new order of things, as being not above half a
clergyman.   As he rises in years and repute he
becomes a rural dean, and exercises some small
authority out of his own parish, by which, however,

The Parson of the Parish

"...unquestioned ease over a ruddy fire..."

his character as a parish parson, pure and simple, is somewhat damaged. He is great in the management of his curate, and arrives at such perfection in his professional career that he inspires his clerk with mingled awe and affection.

Such is the English parish parson, as he was almost always some fifty years since, as he is still in many parishes, but as he will soon cease to become. The homes of such men are among the pleasantest in the country, just reaching in well-being and abundance that point at which perfect comfort exists and magnificence has not yet begun to display itself. And the men themselves have no superiors in their adaptability to social happiness. How pleasantly they talk when the room is tiled, and the outward world is shut out for the night! How they delight in the modest pleasures of the table, sitting in unquestioned ease over a ruddy fire, while the bottle stands ready to the grasp, but not to be grasped too frequently or too quickly. Methinks the eye of no man beams so kindly on me as I fill my glass for the third time after dinner as does the eye of the parson of the parish.

VI.

THE TOWN INCUMBENT.

DR. JOHNSON tells us that an incumbent is he who is in present possession of a benefice, and by quoting Swift shows us that, though in possession of a benefice, the incumbent may be in possession of very little benefit from his benefice. "In many places," Swift says, as quoted by Johnson, "the whole ecclesiastical dues are in lay hands, and the incumbent lieth at the mercy of his patron." The word, therefore, is legitimately used in its ecclesiastical sense, and can apparently be legitimately used in no other sense; but, nevertheless, it has no pleasantly ecclesiastical flavour, and carries with itself none of that acknowledged right to respect which is attached to other clerical titles. To be

named as a curate is almost better than to be named
as an incumbent; for the curate is supposed to be
young, and is on his proper road to higher church
grades, whereas the incumbent is one who has obtained
his promotion, but who is, after all, only an—incumbent.   Every parish parson in the kingdom is no
doubt an incumbent, but in ordinary parlance we
hardly apply the name to the country rector or to the
vicar blessed with a pleasant parsonage.   The incumbent, as we generally recognize him, is a clergyman
who has obtained a town district, who has a church
of his own therein from whence he draws what income
he may make, chiefly by the letting of sittings, and is
so called simply because no other clerical title seems
properly to belong to him.   No clerical aspirant
would be an incumbent,—so to be called,—who
could become a parson proper.

The town incumbent, therefore, is rarely a man
well to do in the world. He is one who earns
his bread hardly in the sweat of his brow, and
too often earns but very poor bread. It is not he
who has married or who will marry the bishop's
daughter.   Indeed, before he becomes a town in-

cumbent he has generally put himself beyond such promotion as that by marrying the girl of his heart without a penny. Had he not done so, and thus become terribly in want of an income,—an income at once, though it be a small income,—he would not have taken a district church, and have submitted his neck to the yoke of town incumbency. He knows that in doing so he is consenting to place himself in that branch of his profession which is the least honoured, though not perhaps the least honourable. He is subjecting himself to the heaviest clerical work with but a small prospect of large clerical loaves or fine clerical fishes; and he is prepared to live in a much lower social rank than that which is enjoyed by his more fortunate brothers in the country. The country parson is all but the squire's equal,—is below the squire in parish standing only as a younger brother is below his elder; but the town incumbent is not equal to the town mayor, and in the estimation of many of his fellow-townsmen is hardly superior to the town beadle. Indeed, he is too often simply recognized as the professional gentleman who has taken his family into the last built new house in

Albert Terrace. There, in Albert Terrace, he looks out upon a brickfield, and writes his sermons with very little of that prestige which belongs to the genuine British parson of the parish. His flock are his hearers, not his parishioners. They sit under him, some because his district church of St. Mary is the nearest to them, some because the sittings at St. Mary's are 5*s*. 6*d*. a year cheaper than they are at the next place of worship,—for St. Mary's is a place of worship rather than a church to the minds of the townsmen,—and some because they prefer his preaching to the preaching of another town incumbent. They sit under him, but they are not his people jure divino, for him to deal with them concerning their eternal welfare as he may please. He does not even know the name of the man who lives next door to him in Albert Terrace; whereas the true parson of the parish knows every detail as to every child born within his domain. The one is simply the town incumbent of St. Mary's as another man may be an attorney, and a third an apothecary; whereas the rural parson is the per-sonage of his parish.

To the position of the town incumbent are attached
none of those half-barbarous but picturesque circumstances which still make the position of our country
parsons almost unintelligible to the inquiring foreigner.
One clergyman, with little or nothing to do in his
parish, has fifteen hundred a year and a beautiful
house for doing that little,—which after all is done
by a curate ; while his neighbour in the next parish
with four times the area and eight times the population, receives one hundred and fifty pounds a year in
lieu of the little tithes ! And yet neither does the
one feel himself to have been unduly favoured, nor
does the other think himself to be injured ! Such
are the more-than-half-barbarous, but still picturesque
circumstances of our rural parishes. But there is
nothing either barbarous or picturesque about the
town incumbent. He has allotted to him a district,
with such or such a population,—a certain number
of thousands over whom it must be much beyond his
power to achieve anything approaching to a pastoral
surveillance,—with a church in the middle of it, and
an income which will fluctuate as the seats in it may
be full or empty. Here, in this arrangement, all the

principles of political economy are kept in view. Here
are supply and demand. Those who want him will
come to him and pay him,—as they do to the baker
or the dentist. If they don't think he suits them,
they will leave him,—as also in similar circumstances they leave their baker and their dentist. If
he can fill his church he will live well and become
sleek. If his gifts in preaching are small, or if his
piety be unrecognized and his labours disregarded,
he will live badly and his outward man will become
rusty. Among town incumbents the rusty greatly
exceed the sleek in numbers.

The town incumbent of whom we are here speaking generally finds himself located among the growing
outskirts of a manufacturing town. Here he sees the
world increasing around him with wonderful rapidity,
and sees also much of the success of the world. The
man who began his struggle in life as a manufacturer,
when he, the incumbent, also began his struggle,
soon rises from step to step, adding chimney to
chimney, and buys his villa residence and sets up
his carriage. In his career, failure was, of course,
possible, but the road to success was open to him,

and has been quickly reached. This his neighbour,
the clergyman, sees, and tells himself, not without
bitterness, that for him there is no such road. For
him there must always be poverty and hard work,
—that worst of all poverty which has to hide itself
under a black coat, and work which is not only cease-
less, but too often thankless and apparently without
adequate result ! This must be his lot in life, he
tells himself,—unless he can preach himself into a
reputation. If he can do that, if he can be a M'Neale
or an English Ward Beecher, then, indeed, there
will be a career open to him. Then he will be sleek,
and people will ask him to dinner, and the wife
of his bosom will hold up her head among other
dames, and his name will become familiar in the
columns of newspapers. This after all is what men
want, town incumbents as well as others ; and so the
town incumbent sets himself to work to make a
reputation for himself by pulpit eloquence. As he
walks along the dull new streets of his district he
fills himself with this ambition, and declares to himself that he will be great as a preacher. He will fill
his seats, and draw men to him,—or, if not men,

at least women. He will denounce sins with a loud
voice and eager accents. And he will denounce
not only sins, but heresies also, and lax doctrines.
By denouncing simply sin few clerical aspirants have
become noted among their neighbours, but the man
who will denounce his neighbours' opinions as well as
his sins will become famous. And so the town incumbent settles himself to his desk and goes to work.

It will be said, no doubt, that a monstrous accusation is here brought against a body of men who
are very eager in doing good works. It is not meant
as any accusation. No charge is intended to be
made against town incumbents, or against any
clergyman, in the description here given. They
endeavour simply to succeed in their profession, as
every man blessed with activity will attempt to
succeed in his profession if it be one in which there
is room for success. Given the church to fill, and
the incumbency to be made valuable by filling it,
and it is simply human nature that an energetic
man shall endeavour to fill his church and make
his profession valuable. He cannot fill his church
by visiting the poor. He cannot earn for himself

even a decent position in the district in which he lives by a careful performance of ordinary clerical duties. If he simply reads the services and officiates at the communion table, and preaches drowsy sermons, he will starve on some 200*l.* a year, and never get his head above water, either as regards money or reputation. Of course he will do his best for himself, and of course he will teach himself to believe that in doing so he is doing the best for the cause which he really loves in his heart. He is not a bad man, or a hypocrite, because he denounces heresies and lax doctrines in a loud voice, instead of endeavouring to teach his people simply that they should not lie, or get drunk, or steal. He is probably a very good man; but he is a good man who would like to have 1,000*l.* a year and a name, instead of 200*l.* a year and no name at all.

But he probably fails. It is sad to say it, and sad to think of it, but failure is the ordinary lot of man. A few among us do advance far enough in the accomplishment of their aspirations to merit the reputation of success, and they are heard of in the world; but the mass of men strive for a while to

The Town Incumbent

"...sleepless nights in the composition of his sermons."

do something, and then sink down into the common ruck, finding the struggle to be too hard for them. They earn bread and live ; and at last, perhaps, are contented. So it is with the town incumbent. He preaches for a while with all his force. He spends sleepless nights in the composition of his sermons. He becomes bolder and bolder in his denouncings. But it is of no avail. He has not the gift of pouring forth either honey or liquid fire from his lips, and his energy is all wasted. He throws himself in despair on the bosom of his wife, who alone has believed in him, and declares that his people have adders' ears and hearts of stone. From that time forth, with saddened spirit and heart all sick within him, he trudges on upon his daily round of duties, not cursing the day, but reviling the day with an asperity purely clerical, on which he became—a town incumbent.

But it is possible that he does not fail. There are, no doubt, town incumbents who succeed in preaching themselves into fortunes and reputations, and who become very sleek and very famous, who are able to mount higher than their pulpits, on to platforms, and can then enjoy the inestimable privilege of abusing their opponents without fear of reply. But, of all clergymen, the successful town preacher seems to be the farthest removed from those clerical excellences of charity and good-will among men, and the farthest also from those special clerical duties for which our clergy are most valued. They will preach;—yes, by the hour together! Nine times a week we have heard of such a one preaching, and have then known him to speak of himself as a martyr in the service! But they will do nothing else.

For the unsuccessful town incumbent we all of us have sympathy. His work is hard, his payment is small, and his lines have fallen to him in unpleasant places. But for the successful town incumbent, for the clergyman who fills his church with prayerful, tearful, excitable, but at the same time remunerative ladies, few men can have any sympathy.

The position of the town incumbent is not, in truth, in unison with the Church of England as established among us. The glory of the English parson is that his position is ensured to him whether he satisfies those whom he is called upon to serve, or whether he does not satisfy them. Consequently he can be, and is, independent of his congregation. He will wish of course to be on pleasant terms with them, but it will not be for his pocket's sake. And it seems that such independence as this is essential to the position of a clergyman of the Church of England. It is doubtless true that the number of rural rectors and vicars among us will never be increased, whereas the number of town incumbents will continue to increase from year to year. As the population grows, so will their number grow. But it is to be hoped that the peculiar evils of their position may be remedied by altered arrangements as to their income. If this be not possible, or be not done, we shall hardly find that sons of English gentlemen will continue to seek the Church as a profession.

VII.

THE COLLEGE FELLOW WHO HAS TAKEN ORDERS.

In speaking of a college fellow, a fellow of a college at Oxford or Cambridge is the fellow of whom we intend to speak. There may, probably, be other fellowships going in these prolific days, as there are other universities, and degrees given by other academical bodies; but we will claim, for the moment, to belong to the old school in such matters, and will recognize as college fellows only those who are presented to us as fellows by the two great sister universities.

When a man becomes a fellow various possessions and privileges are conferred upon him, such as a certain income, a certain rank in his college,

a residence within his college, and a place at the
high table in hall; and among these privileges
and possessions is the great privilege—of a title
to orders.   In respect to some fellowships this
privilege may be enjoyed or neglected according to
the will of the individual fellow.   In respect to
others the fellow must avail himself of it, and
must become a clergyman, if not absolutely at once,
then within a short period of his election.   And
there is a third condition, such as that which prevails at the greatest of all our colleges, namely,
Trinity, Cambridge, in accordance with which certain
years of grace are allowed, and a fellow may remain
a fellow for a period of years without taking orders.
But, as we believe, at all these colleges a fellowship
confers a title to orders,—the right, that is, on
the part of the fellow to demand ordination from
the bishop; and, as a rule, this privilege is enjoyed.
As we are dealing in these sketches with none
but clergymen, the fellow who has availed himself
of this title is the fellow whom we will keep in view.

All our readers will know what is meant by
taking orders,—the process by which a layman

becomes a deacon or a priest under the bishop's hands; and most of them will understand that a title to orders is the possession in prospect of such sacerdotal position as will justify a bishop in turning a layman into a clergyman. Thus, for instance, a man has a title to orders who can show that there is a living waiting for his enjoyment and for his services. The offer of a curacy confers a title, and this is the title by which the great body of aspirants to the sacerdotal profession claim their right to admission. Such claimants the bishop is bound to ordain, providing that they show themselves to be fit;—but without a title, or recognized place of clerical duty ready for the candidate as soon as he shall become a clergyman, no bishop will ordain any one. And among other titles there is the title conferred by a college fellowship. The fellow of a college goes before a bishop demanding to be ordained simply because he is a fellow,—and the bishop ordains him. It is a great privilege, for that man is Reverend from that time forth for evermore. In all future ages he will be written down as having been Reverend.

There can be no doubt that when this pleasant arrangement became a portion of college law there was good reason for it. The colleges were ecclesiastical bodies, generally if not entirely under ecclesiastical governance, and a fellow not an ecclesiastic would have been very much in the way at most of them. Men who were clergymen, and men who were not, differed much more strongly then than they do now, both as to the inner life of the man and the outward appearance of the man. And it was then recognized as a part of the great Church system of the day, that in many places ecclesiastics, who were of course unmarried, should live together, passing their time in that state which was then considered to be for them the most salutary and to others the most useful,—saying prayers for the laity which the laity could hardly be got to say for themselves, and maintaining by their continued presence at the universities something of the result of their education, and some show of learning and piety. In those days the fellows of our colleges were monks of a favoured order,—especially favoured because they were, or were presumed to be, especially learned. Looking at our Church, our colleges, and our religion, as they then existed, we shall feel little doubt as to the propriety of fellows having been clergymen in those days. But now,—now that things are so much altered in our Church and in our colleges and in our religion,—sometimes a doubt does creep upon us as to the expediency of this title to orders which a fellowship conveys, and the use which is made of this title.

In the Roman Catholic Church worship seems to have been ordained for the gratification of God. The people were, and indeed are still, taught that God and his saints like prayers and incense and church services, and will reward those who are liberal in bestowing them. It is, therefore, natural that in the Church of Rome there should be,—or, more natural still, that there should have been when this idea was more prevalent in Roman Catholic countries than it is now,—legions of priests whose church administrations were performed with a view to their effect on the Creator, and with no view to any effect on man. But in Protestant countries worship is used, as we suppose, simply for the use of man. It is the duty of the clergyman, as clergyman, to assist other men in worshipping rather than to achieve anything by worship on his own part. If such be the case,—and such appears to be at any rate the existing theory of our own Protestant Church,—it is difficult to conceive how any man can become a clergyman of the Church of England who has no intention whatsoever of helping others to worship,—who has not before him any prospect of performing the duties of a clergyman.

It will be said, doubtless, that the statement here made is wrong and untrue, because the clerical fellow of a college has always before him the prospect of succeeding to a college living, and does generally end his days as the parson of a parish to which he has been presented by his college in the regular order of good things accruing to him. It is quite true that the clerical fellow does in this way become a real clergyman, or a parson proper if I may so call him, in the latter half of his life, when at forty or forty-five he begins to feel that he would like to have something softer near to him than his gyp or laundrywoman, and bethinks himself of some Eliza whom he has long half loved, but would never before allow himself to love altogether,—because of his fellowship. The fellow then drops his fellowship, and takes a living, and goes to his parish and becomes a real clergyman. But the fact that he does so offers only another and a stronger objection to his original ordination, while it does not, in truth, at all invalidate that already stated. It is true that the fellow becomes a clergyman at last; but who will maintain that any man has fitly used a profession to which he has never applied himself during those years of his life in which his energy was the strongest, and which he embraced without any view to using it at all? The fellow of a college is ordained in order that he may hold his fellowship, — because in old days, when the fellowship was instituted, fellows were supposed to live the life of monks. We do not think that any existing fellow of a college at Oxford or Cambridge will declare that he has undergone ordination with an express view to the living to which he may succeed after ten or fifteen years.

And now we will venture to say a few words as to that stronger objection to the practice of ordaining fellows which we maintain is to be found in this

practice of their succeeding to college livings by
rotation. When we employ a doctor or a lawyer or
an architect, we select a man who knows his profession, and who has proved that he knows it by his
practice. Young men entering these professions
make their way upwards to that reputation which
will bring them practice by attaching themselves to
those who are older and more experienced, or by
consenting to practise for a while, as it were, experi-
mentally, without much view to income. And in the
Church generally the same order of things prevails.
It is admitted on all hands within the church, by
bishops, by archdeacons, by all working parish
clergymen,—by all men who have interested themselves on the subject,—that the only fit education
for a parish parson is to be found in a parish curacy.
As a man to be a good bishop should have been a
parish parson, so to be a good parson a man should
have been a curate. That we take to be good clergyman's law; but that law is infringed on every occasion
on which a college living is taken by a resident college
fellow. A college fellow may, of course, become a
curate, and when such a one succeeds to his living

all is well. But the man who does so should have
been ordained on the title of his curacy, not on the
title of his fellowship.

Does any man believe that that very pleasant
fellow whom he has known at college, and who has
sparkled so brightly in common room, who has been
so energetic in the management of the college
finances, and in the reform of college abuses,—who
has gradually succeeded during his fifteen years of
residence in putting off all those outward clerical
symbols which as a novice he found himself con-
strained to adopt, and who during his annual visit to
London has become a well-instructed man of the
world,—can any one, we say, believe that such a one
at the age of forty can be fit to go into a parish and
undertake the cure of the parochial souls? There
are, we fancy, some who do so believe ; but they are
those who think that nothing is necessary to make a
parson but orders and a living,—that the profession
of a clergyman is unlike any other trade or calling
known, requiring for the due performance of its duties
no special fitness, no training, no skill, no practice,
no thought, and no preparation.

The College Fellow who has taken Orders
"who has so brightly sparkled in common room..."

The Reverend Joseph Brown stands senior on the list of the fellows of St. Lazarus, within the walls of which happy institution he has lived as fellow and bursar for the last thirty years. No man understands better than the Reverend Joseph Brown the proper temperature of port wine, or the amount of service which a college servant should render. But at the age of fifty-five he falls into unexpectedly tender relations with an amiable female, and on that account he undertakes the pastoral care of the souls of the parish of Eiderdown ! What if Eiderdown got its doctor in the same way, or its butcher ? What if the ladies of Eiderdown were bound to employ a milliner sent to them after some such fashion ? But no man or woman can conceive the possibility of any workman presuming to attempt to earn his bread by his work after such a fashion as this,—excepting always a clergyman. In the Church, because it is so picturesque and well-beloved in its old-fashioned garments, we can put up with anomalies which elsewhere would be unendurable. A bishop uses his patronage as personal property, and college fellows become clergymen and succeed to livings by right, as though in this business of the cure of souls, and in this business only, there were no necessity for that progress in skill and efficiency which all other callings demand! There was a time when men became captains of ships and colonels of regiments in much the same way; but the picturesque absurdities of the army and navy were less endearing than those of the Church, and they therefore have been made to succumb.

It will probably be admitted that the Reverend Joseph Brown, much as he was liked by all who knew him at St. Lazarus, and much as he was respected by those who were brought into collegiate relations with him, was not the very best pastor whom the Church of England could have given to the people of Eiderdown; but many who will admit this will still think that in being ordained as a young man on the title of his fellowship, he did that which was becoming to him as one who had passed through his university education with honour and success. Fellows of colleges always have been clergymen, holding high characters as such in their profession, and why not the Reverend Joseph Brown? Is it not

also known to us that such a man, located as a
bachelor in his college, is more likely to lead a good
and sober life as a clergyman than he would do as a
layman? Such, probably, would be the arguments
used in defence of clerical fellowships; and we will
admit that the Reverend Joseph Brown has throughout his whole career given support to such arguments
by his conduct. But yet he has never in truth been
a clergyman. Though an ordained priest, he has
done no priestly work, and has always been somewhat angry when any one has suggested to him that
he should take a part in any clerical duties. At
first, indeed, he was somewhat careful in maintaining
outward clerical symbols, and was occasionally anx-
ious to feed himself with inward clerical thoughts,
having been moved thereto by the terrible earnestness of his ordination,—by the solemnity of a ceremony which, though he had determined to regard it
simply as the means of placing him in the possession
of certain temporal advantages, so impressed itself
upon him as being personal to himself, that he could
not at once escape from its bonds. But gradually
he overcame that weakness, and found himself

enabled to live, as any other gentleman might live, an easy pleasant life, with nothing of the clergyman about him but the word Reverend attached to his name on his cards and letters. The colour of his lower vestments approaches perhaps nearer to black than it would have done had he not been so encumbered, and men in the world at large are perhaps a little less free in their remarks before him than they would be before other men. This he regrets painfully; but it is all that he has to regret. The fellows, his predecessors in the old days,—who were, in fact, monks as well as fellows,—were called upon to live in accordance with certain monastic and ascetic rules, which they either obeyed to their supposed glory, or disobeyed to their supposed peril. Matins, lauds, nones, vespers, complines, and what not, were their lot,—and came upon them heavily enough, no doubt, if they did their duty; but now-a-days we do not care much, even at our universities, for lauds and complines. Undergraduates indeed must "keep" so many chapels a week, but the clerical fellow is under no such bond. Even if he were under such bond he could say his prayers in his college chapel as well as a layman as he can as a clergyman. And one may suppose that as a layman he would abstain from doing so when the opportunity is provided with an easier conscience than he can have as a priest. But his conscience is easy, because he knows that in fact he is no clergyman. He has simply undergone a certain ceremony in order that he may enjoy his fellowship,—and hereafter take a living should the amiable and tender relationship of matrimony fall in his way.

VIII.

THE CURATE IN A POPULOUS PARISH.

WOULD that it were possible to enforce upon the bishops, as a part of their duty, the task of furnishing annually a statistical return which should show what proportion of the clerical duties in their dioceses was done by curates, and what proportion by other clergymen ; and also what payment had been made to the curates for the work so done, and what payment to those who were not curates. Such statement might show us for instance, in a tabulated form, how many morning services and how many evening services had been performed by each curate, how many sermons preached by him, how many children baptized, how many dead men buried, how many marriages celebrated, and, above all, how many cottages visited.

Then, if we could see, together with all this, what amount of the payment received could be justly appropriated to each task performed, we should have some clear idea of the manner in which the revenues of the Church are divided among those who do the work of the Church. We all know that no such statistical information is within our reach. The bishops are altogether beyond our power, and cannot be ordered by any one to do anything. The idea of comparing the work done with the payment given for the work would be horrible to the imagination of every beneficed clergyman in the Church of England. It would be horrible even to the imagination of the curates themselves, who, like the needy knifegrinder, have no adequate conception of the injustice they are themselves suffering; and who are, as a body, so well inclined towards the rules and traditions of the profession to which they belong, that they have not as yet taught themselves to wish for a change. No clergyman in our Church has, as yet, taken it into his head that there should be any analogy, or any proportion, between work and wages in his profession, as there is such analogy and such proportion in all other professions. There is a something of revolutionary tendency in the suggestion that clergymen should be paid in accordance with their work, which is almost profane to the mind of a clergyman, and which vexes him sorely as being subversive of that grand position which he holds as the owner of a temporal freehold. The very irregularity of the payments still made to parish parsons, and formerly made to bishops, half justifies a latent idea that clergymen, though they work and receive payment, are not labourers working for hire. A second son inherits his living as the elder son inherits his estate;—and the rector who receives his living from his bishop is equally firm in his possession. He may be blessed with 1,000*l.* a year for doing very little, or have 200*l.* a year for doing a great deal; but in either case what he receives has no connection with what he does, and therefore no such statistics as those of which we have spoken can be supplied. No revelation will be made to us tending in any degree to give us the information for which we ask.

That there will come an adjustment between work and wages in the Church, as in all other professions, is certain. Indeed, much has been done towards this adjustment already, though not after the fashion above proposed. The incomes of all bishops have been arranged on such an idea,—to the great detriment, as has before been explained, of episcopal magnificence. Deans and canons have fallen beneath the levelling hands of ecclesiastico-political economists. And out of the funds which have been acquired by these adjustments and curtailings of ecclesiastical wealth, certain incumbents working in populous parishes have received augmentations of pay, making their incomes up to the very modest stipend of 300*l*. per annum. But nothing in all this has touched the great body of the clergymen of the Church of England, or has as yet shown any general recognition of the principle that the hire of the labourer should be proportioned to the labour done.

In speaking of the work and wages of curates, it must of course be admitted that in all professions and all trades the beginner should be contented to work his way up, taking at first, and being contented to take, a modest remuneration for the very best that he can do. The young barrister does not get fifty-guinea fees at once, nor does the young medical practitioner jump at once into the good graces of the old ladies and gentlemen who make the fortunes of mature doctors ; but at the bar, and in the profession of physic, there is at least some proportion kept. The man who gets the most money is generally the hardest-worked man ;—or if, in some cases, it be not so, the lower man who works harder than him above him receives something like a fair share of the spoil. If he be successful in work he is successful in pay also. Being successful in work, he will not work without success in pay. But the curate, let his success in work be what it may, does not even think that he has, on that account, a claim to proportionate remuneration. If he can get to the soft side of his bishop, if he have an aunt that knows some friend of the Lord Chancellor, or a father who has means to buy a living for him,—and he be not himself of too tender a conscience in the matter of simony,— then he may hope to rise. But of rising in his profession because he is fit to rise he has no hope. The idea has not, as yet, come home to him that he

has a positive claim upon his bishop because he has
worked hard and honestly in his profession.

It is notorious that a rector in the Church of
England, in the possession of a living of, let us say,
a thousand a year, shall employ a curate at seventy
pounds a year, that the curate shall do three-fourths
or more of the work of the parish, that he shall
remain in that position for twenty years, taking
one-fourteenth of the wages while he does three-
fourths of the work, and that nobody shall think
that the rector is wrong or the curate ill-used! All
the world,—that is to say, the rector's friends and
the curate's friends also,—have been so long accus-
tomed to this state of things, the bishops have had it
so long under their eyes, the idea of a temporal freehold in a living being a good thing for the parson
instead of a good thing for the parishioner has got
such a hold of us all,—that we none of us see the
injustice of the present practice, or stop to inquire
how it grew up among us, originating in a practice
that was not unjust. When the rectors and vicars
were very many among us in comparison to the
curates, when a curate was needed in but few parishes,

—the ordinary tenure of a curacy was, of course, short. There have been instances, no doubt, since the earliest years in which curates were employed, of curates who have remained curates till they were old men ; but the succession from the smaller number of the inferior grade to the much larger number of the superior grade was, of course, rapid, and a clerical babe would be contented to take a curacy even at seventy pounds a year, who might reasonably expect to be raised from that humble position after a service of two or three years. But now-a-days, since the immense increase of population has forced upon us an increase of curates,—any increase in the number of endowed rectors and vicars being out of our reach, —the clerical babe must become a clerical old man on the same pittance, and it is coming to pass that young men whose friends have been at the trouble of giving them a good education, do not like the prospect of becoming curates, without any prospect of rising from their curacies to the glories and comforts of full-blown parsondom.

And in considering this matter we must remember that the curate of to-day is deprived of a great advan-

tage which belonged as a matter of course to the
curate of yesterday. The latter was presumed to be,
by virtue of his calling, a gentleman, and as such
possessed almost a right to be admitted into society
which neither his fortune nor his own abilities would
have opened to him. He was a gentleman as it were
by Act of Parliament, and it was understood that he
might receive where he could not give, and so enjoy
many of those good things which a liberal income
produces, though such things were beyond the reach
of his own purse. Thus the pains of his position
were mitigated. And in this way the poor clergyman
mixed with men who were not poor, and received
a something from his status in the world, to which
no disgrace was attached, though it was something
which he could not return. But we may say that all
this is now altered. A clergyman is no longer a
gentleman by Act of Parliament. Till the other day
he was admitted into all families simply because he
had a place in the reading-desk of the parish church;
—but he is no longer so admitted. Things have
become changed within a few years, and mothers are
becoming as chary of admitting the curate among their

flocks—till they know exactly what are the curate's
bearings—as they have ever been in regard to the
new young doctor till they have known his bearings.
Under these circumstances, all men who care for the
Church of England are beginning to ask themselves
how the race of curates is to be continued.

Let us for a moment look at the life of a curate
of the present day. We will suppose that he comes
from some college at Cambridge or Oxford. We will
so suppose because Cambridge and Oxford still give
us the majority of our clergymen, though we can
hardly hope that they will long continue to be so
bountiful. He enters the Church, moved to do so
by what we all call a special vocation. During the
period of his education he feels himself to be warmed
towards the teaching of the English Protestant
Church, and as he finds the ministry easily in his
way he enters it—and at about the age of twenty-four
he becomes a curate. He is at first gratified at the
ease with which are confided to him the duties of an
assistant in the cure of souls, and does not think
much of the stipend which is allotted to him. He
has lived as a boy at the university upon two hundred

a year without falling much into debt, and thinks
that as a man he can live easily upon seventy pounds.
Hitherto he has indulged himself with many things.
He has smoked cigars, and had his wine parties, and
been luxurious ; but as a curate he will be delighted
to deny himself all luxuries. His heart will be in
the service of his God, and his appetites shall be to
him as thorns which he will make to crackle in the
fire. To eat bread without butter and to drink tea
without milk is a glory to him,—and so he begins
the world.

And for a year or two, if he be not weak-minded,
things do not go badly with him. The parson's wife
sees far into his character, and is kind to him, stirred
thereto by a conviction of which she is herself unconscious, that the money payment made by her
husband is insufficient.. The dry bread and the
brown tea are still sweetened by reminiscences of St.
Paul's sufferings, and the young man consoles himself by inward whisperings of forty stripes save one
five times repeated. To be persecuted is as yet sweet
to him, and he knows that in doing all the rector's
work for seventy pounds a year he is being per-

secuted. But anon there grows up within his breast
a feeling in which the grievance as regards this world
is brought into unpleasant contact with the persecu-
tion in which he has a pietistic delight. He still
rejoices in the reflection that he cannot possibly buy
for himself a much-needed half-dozen of new shirts,
but is uncomfortably angry because the rector himself
is not only idle, but has bought a new carriage.
And then he gives way a little—the least in the
world—and at the end of the year owes the butcher
a small bill which he cannot settle. From that day
the vision of St. Paul melts before his eyes, and he
sighs for replenished fleshpots.

But he still works hard in his curacy,—perhaps
harder than ever, driven thereto by certain inward
furies. What will become of him,—of him, with his
seventy pounds a year, and nothing further to expect
as professional result, if he be deserted by his religious ecstasy? But religious ecstasy will not permit
itself to be maintained on such terms, and gradually
there creeps upon him the heart-breaking disappointment of a soured and an injured man. In the midst
of this he takes to himself a wife. It is always so.

The Curate in a Populous Parish

"...a much needed half-dozen of new shirts..."

The man who is most in the dark will be the best inclined to take a leap in the dark. In the lowest period of his despondency he becomes a married man —enjoying at the moment a little fitful gleam of shortlived worldly pleasure. Then, again, he is a male saint for a few months, with a female saint beside him ; and after that all collapses, and he goes down into irrevocable misery and distress. In a few years we know of him as a beggar of old clothes, as a man whom from time to time his friends are asked to lift from unutterable depths of distress by dona- tions which no gentleman can take without a crushed spirit—as a pauper whom the poor around him know to be a pauper, and will not, therefore, respect as a minister of their religion. In all this there has been very little, we may say nothing, of fault in the curate himself. As a young man, almost as a boy, he placed himself in a position of which he knew the old conditions rather than those then existing around him—and through that mistake he fell.

But young men are now beginning to know, and the fathers of young men also, what are at present the true conditions of the Church of England as a profession, and they who have been nurtured softly, and who have any choice, will not undergo its trials —and its injustice! For men of a lower class in life, who have come from harder antecedents, the normal seventy pounds per annum may suffice; but all modern Churchmen will understand what must be the effect on the Church if such be the recruits to which the Church must trust.

IX.

THE IRISH BENEFICED CLERGYMAN.

THE difference between an Irish and an English parson is greater, perhaps, than that which exists between Irishmen and Englishmen of any other special denomination, and is of a nature exactly contrary to that which generally marks the distinctive character of the Milesian and the John Bull. The normal Irishman is a jolly fellow; but the normal Irish Protestant clergyman is a severe, sombre man, one who speaks of life in sad, subdued tones,—unless when he is minatory in the pulpit,—one who looks at things around him with a continual remembrance that life is but a span long, that men are but grass of the field, that the sickle is ready and the oven heated, and that it is worth no man's while to be comfortable here on earth. He is preaching every moment of his life, preaching in his gait, preaching in every tone of his voice, preaching in every act that he does, preaching in every turn of his eyes. Find him asleep, and you will find him preaching with a long-protracted, indignant, low-church, Protestant snore, very eloquent as to the scarlet woman. But an English parson, let him be ever so much given to preaching, preaches only from his pulpit. He may scold, advise, or cajole in the school, the cottage, or the drawing-room ; but he keeps his sermons for his Sunday work. An Irish clergyman does not shake hands with you without leaving a text or two in your palm,—with his own special comments on their tenour as regards the Pope.

The reason of this is not far to seek. The Irish clergyman does not live in the midst of Protestants with whom he sympathizes, but is surrounded by Roman Catholics with whom he cannot sympathize, and against whom he is driven to feel almost a personal enmity, not only by reason of their creed which he sorely hates, but by reason also of the anomalies of his own position which are so hateful to them. He is always in a state of feud,—in a state

of feud, not only against the devil, as should be the
case with all of us whether clergymen or laymen, but
against Antichrist on the Seven Hills, against the
scarlet woman who goes about devouring, against the
Pope who is to him a ravenous old woman as to whom
he cannot say whether he is most ravenous or most
old-womanish, against a creed which has for him
none of the attractions of Christianity,—in which he
sees only the small points of divergence from his own,
and which is, therefore, worse to him than the creed
of Mussulman or of Jew. He is therefore always
serious, as is a soldier who is ever buckling on his
armour, and somewhat sad, as is a soldier who cannot
get his enemy down so that he may take away his
standard and trample on him. The Irish Protestant
clergyman is ever longing to lead troops of the Roman
Catholics of Ireland in triumph to the top of the
Tarpeian rock of conversion; but they succeed in
bringing thither but one and another, and these one
and another are such that they hardly grace the
chariot wheels of their victors.

The popular idea of an Irish clergyman in
England is, we think, somewhat incorrect. He is

often supposed to be an idle man, listless for want of occupation, given to self-indulgence, ill-educated, eager only in defence of his temporalities, and warmly attached to the party politics of Protestants, rather than to their religion. Such men may doubtless be found among the holders of livings in Ireland, as they may also in England; but such is not the general character of the Irish clergyman. He is a man always active, though unfortunately his activity has but small field of usefulness. His air is not the air of a listless man, but of a man disappointed,—as it may well be. As he goes on in life he may come to love too dearly his slippers and his armchair, and perhaps to feel, as disappointed men will feel,—will feel but not acknowledge,—that the consolations of the dinner-table are, and that none others are, reliable ; but such is not his normal condition of body or mind. I will not say that he is generally well-educated,—because the word means so much. But the Irish clergyman has generally read as much as his brother in England, though his reading has been of a different nature. Of reading applicable specially to his own profession he has

probably endured more than his brother in England.
In short he is more of a clergyman and less of a man
of the world than the English parson,—with this
misfortune, that his clerical activities are always at
work against enemies and not on behalf of friends.

There would not be space for me to say much, in
this short sketch, of the now acknowledged anomalies
of the position of the Church of England as
established in Ireland; but I will endeavour to
describe the outward form and bearing of the
clergyman whom these anomalies have produced,
begging my readers to believe at the outset that
the Irish clergyman may be regarded, nine times out
of ten,—ninety-nine out of a hundred I think we
might say,—as a sincere man, as a man with strong
convictions, who has no shadow of doubt in his own
mind that the surest road to heaven, if not the only
one, is by that special pathway of which he professes
to have the clue. There is no reservation within his
mind, as to his religion with its intricacies being good
for the ignorant, for instance, though perhaps not
altogether needed for the educated. He has no
doubts. The Eureka with him is a certainty. That

men will be saved and will be damned as they live remote from or attached to papistical teachings is to him a reality. Now it is something that a man should be capable of a sincere belief, and that he should succeed in attaining to it.

The Irish beneficed clergyman has almost always been educated at Trinity, Dublin, and has there been indoctrinated with those high Protestant principles with which he has before been inoculated. He is, of course, the son of an Irish Protestant gentleman, and has therefore sucked them in with his mother's milk. He goes before his Protestant bishop and takes his orders with a corps of other young men exactly similarly circumstanced. And thus he has never had given to him an opportunity of rubbing his own ideas against those of men who have been educated with different proclivities. He has never lived at college either with Roman Catholics, or with Presbyterians, or with Protestants of a sort different from his sort. In his cradle, at his father's table, at school, at the university, in all the lessons that he has learned, in all the games that he has played, in his converse with his sisters, in his first soft, faint, whisperings with his sisters' friends, in his loud unreserved talkings with his closest companions, the same two ideas, cheek by jowl, have ever been present to him,— the State ascendancy of his own Church, and the numerical superiority of another Church antagonistic to his own. When we consider all this, and look at the training which the Irish clergyman has undergone, how can we wonder at his idiosyncrasies?

Irish clergymen are thus bound together more closely than clergymen in England, chiefly from the want of opportunity for divergence. Not only education goes always in the same course, but the circumstances of professional career attach themselves very closely to one form. The livings are more generally in the gift of the bishops than with us, and the Irish bishops, perhaps, are more inclined to give promotion solely on the score of merit than are the English bishops. There is, we believe, less of Church patronage,—or rather of the exercise of Church patronage for the furthering of private ends; and if this be so, the Irish Church in that respect is superior to our own. But as the Irish curate is to get his living from the Irish bishop, and is to receive it as a reward for his clerical zeal, and not because he is his father's son, it is absolutely incumbent on him to work as a curate up to the established diocesan mark. And this mark or standard will not be the standard fixed exactly by the bishop himself. Bishop's predecessors and bishop's chaplains, and the very air round the bishop's residence, will have been for years impregnated with high Protestant principles. And even a bishop who may himself be lacking in that fiery Protestant zeal which is regarded as Church of England orthodoxy in Ireland, will not find himself able to subdue the strength of the atmosphere in which he is called upon to live. There have been bishops sent to Ireland,—nay, there still are bishops in Ireland, placed over dioceses there because they have been considered to be,—we will not say anti-Protestant, but liberal in their tendencies towards Roman Catholics and Presbyterians; but the clergymen who come forth ordained from under the hands of the liberal Whatelys are nearly of the same form as those who, from time out of mind, have been given to us by the orthodox Trenches and the orthodox Beresfords. The stream runs too strongly to be

stemmed by any bishop;—so that the Irish clergyman
who desires to swim must, almost of necessity, swim
with it.

The clerical aspirant becomes first a curate. One
would be disposed to think that there could be no
great need for curates in Ireland,—that as the population of the country is chiefly Roman Catholic, and
as not much above one-half even of the Protestants
conforms to the Church of England,—so that the
proportion of even nominal church-goers is less than
one in eight,—and as there is a beneficed parson in
every parish, whether there be much, little, or nothing
to do,—curates could not be needed in addition to
rectors and vicars ; but curates seem to be as common
in Ireland as they are in England,—the souls of men
requiring, we must suppose, more surveillance, and
the work, we must presume, being more closely done.
The young clergyman almost always becomes a curate,
and then looks to his bishop for a living. Depending
thus on the bishop, he lives strictly, works with
energy, is constant in his adherence to all the exigen-
cies of his cloth, and in the ripeness of time is blessed
with a living of, we will say, two hundred and fifty

pounds a year with a glebe. Irish livings are thought to be very good, but the value here named is above the average. In the rich diocese of Meath, perhaps of all the Irish dioceses the richest, the endowment of more than one-half of the livings is less than the sum above named. Then begins the real battle of his life. Of course our Irish clergyman marries, and of course he has a family, and, even in Ireland, the support of a wife and family upon two hundred and fifty pounds a year is not easy. His glebe is probably remote from any town, and far removed from the houses of other gentry. The parish squire is a personage who, as such, hardly exists in Ireland. Here and there a resident landowner is to be found with a large house and a wide demesne; but the parish squire who has interests in the parish almost identical with those of the parson does not exist. The clergyman, therefore, located in the country lives alone, and his nearest neighbours are the rectors and vicars of other parishes. He lives alone, and the solitude of his life does not tend to make him jovial, or even satisfied with things around him. But he has his religion, and he tells himself that that should suffice for him;—that that

should be all in all to him. He has his religion,
and he endeavours to make the most of it. It is to
be not only his guide through life to things spiritual,
but his chief comfort in things temporal. He must
abide by it in every phase under which it has been
presented to him ; he must hang to it as the politician
does to his party ; he must trust to it,—not merely
for the God and Saviour whom he knows through its
assistance, but for his very politics, thoroughly believing
that all its doctrines and all its formularies are essen-
tially necessary, and that they must be taken with
the exact tenets and with all the twists which have
been given to them by his side in church disputes.

Of all men the Irish beneficed clergyman is the
most illiberal, the most bigoted, the most unforgiving,
the most sincere, and the most enthusiastic. He is
too often an unhappy man, being poor, aggrieved,
soured by the misfortunes of his own position, conscious that something is wrong, though never doubting
that he himself is right, aware of his own unavoidable
idleness, aware that when he works he works to little
or no effect, feeling that prayers said and sermons
preached to his own family, to three policemen and

his clerk, cannot be said to have been preached to much effect. It is a life-long grief to him that in his parish there should be four hundred and fifty nominal Roman Catholics, and only fifty nominal members of the Church of England. But yet he is staunch. There is a good day coming, though he will never see it. He consoles himself as best he may with the certainty of the coming triumph; but cannot refrain from sadness as he tells himself that it certainly will not come in his days.

There is nothing more melancholy to a man's heart, nothing more depressing to his feelings, than a doubt whether or no he truly earns the bread which he eats. The beneficed clergyman of the Church of England in Ireland has no doubt as to his right to his bread,—as to his right either by the law of man or by the law of God; but he cannot but have a doubt as to his earning it. He tells himself that it is the fault of the people,—that it comes of their darkness; that he is there if they will only come to him. But they do not come; and he has on his spirit the terrible weight of wages received without adequate work performed. It is a killing weight.

The Irish Beneficed Clergyman

"...sermons preached to his own family, to three policemen and his clerk..."

To preach to three policemen is as hard as to preach to three hundred educated men and women,—nay, perhaps it is much harder; but he who so preaches feels that his preaching is nothing. He is as the convict labourer who moves sand from one hole to another;—and who can get no comfort from his work.

And he is daily told,—this Irish beneficed clergyman of the Church of England,—that of all men he is the most overpaid. Newspapers which he cannot but see, speakers on public platforms to whose orations he cannot entirely stop his ears, are telling him constantly that he is a drone, growing fat upon honey which he does not help to make, threatening him with Parliamentary annihilation, and invoking against him all the ardour of all the Radicals. In the meantime, he knows that he and his are barely able to subsist on the pittance which the Church allows him. He has terrible temporal grievances in poor rates, charges for his glebe, deductions on this side and on that, till he knows not how to pay his butcher and his baker, and the wife of his bosom is driven to painful, stringent economies. He has not, he tells himself, half of that which a liberal Church in old days had intended for the parish, and yet they tell him that he is robbing the public! He is there to do his duty. Why do not the people come to him? For what he receives, whether it is much or little, he is ready to work, if only his work might be accepted.

But his work is not accepted, and there is no slightest sign in Ireland that it will be accepted. The anomalies of the Church of England in Ireland are terribly distressing, and call aloud for reform. But to none can they be so distressing as to the beneficed clergyman in Ireland; and in the behalf of no other class is that reform so vitally needed.

X. AND LAST.

THE CLERGYMAN WHO SUBSCRIBES FOR COLENSO.

WE have heard much of the Broad Church for many years, till the designation is almost as familiar to our ears as that of the High Church or of the Low Church; but the Broad Church of former times,— some twenty years ago, we will say, when the ecclesiastical world was all on fire because the then Prime Minister was minded to give a mitre to a certain professor of divinity at Oxford,—held doctrines very far indeed behind those to which the liberal parsons of these days have made progress. The ordinary Broad Church clergyman of that era was one who showed himself to be broad by his tolerance of the doubts of others, rather than by the expression of doubts of his own. He was not uncomfortably shocked at finding himself in company with one who was weak in faith as to the Old Testament miracles, and listened with placid equanimity to discussions which went on around him to show that our ancient Bible chronology was defective. But now we have got much beyond that. The liberal clergyman of the Church of England has long since given up Bible chronology, has given up many of the miracles, and is venturing forward into questions the very asking of which would have made the hairs to stand on end on the head of the broadest of the broad in the old days, twenty years since. There are bishops still living, and others have lately died, who must have been astonished to find how quickly their teaching has had its results, how soon the tree has produced its fruit.

The free-thinking clergyman of the present time is to be found more often in London than in the provinces, and more frequently in the towns than in country parishes. They are not many in number, as compared with the numbers of all parsondom in these realms; but they are men of whom we hear much, and they are sufficiently numerous to leaven the whole. There are many things, gone recently altogether out of date, which the meek old-world clergyman dares no longer teach, though he knows not why,—the placid, easy-minded clergyman who would be so well satisfied to teach all that his father taught before him,—the actual six days for instance, the actual and needed rest on the seventh; but the placid clergyman dares not teach them, not knowing why he dares not. He has been leavened unconsciously by the free-thinking of his liberal brother, and his teaching comes forth conformed in some degree to the new doctrines, although, to himself, the feeling is simply that the ground is being cut from under him, and that that special bit of ground, —the actual six days,—has slid away altogether from the touch of his feet.

In London and in the large towns, where they most abound, these new teachers have their own circles, their own flocks, their own churches, and their admirers who have become familiar with them. And it is when so placed, no doubt, that they are most efficacious in operating on the education of laymen and of other clergymen. But it is when such a one finds himself placed as a parson in a country parish, out, as it were, alone among the things of another day, that he calls upon himself the greatest attention. He has around him antediluvian rectors and pietistic vicars, who regard him not only as a bird of prey who has got into a community of domestic poultry, but, worse still, as a bird that is fouling its own nest. They hate his teaching, as all teachers must hate doctrines which are subversive of their own—which, however, they can themselves neither subvert nor approve. But they hate more intensely that want of professional thoroughness, that absence of esprit de corps, which these gentlemen seem to them to exhibit. "He has taken orders," says the antediluvian rector, speaking of his free-thinking neighbour to his confidential friend, "simply to upset the Church! He believes in nothing; nothing in heaven, nothing on earth,—nothing under the earth. He told his people yesterday that the Book of Exodus is an old woman's story. And the worst of it is, we cannot do anything to get rid of him ;—no, by Heaven, not anything!" To which the rector's confidential friend replies that the rector has still the power left of preaching his own doctrine. "Psha!" says the rector, "preach, indeed! Preach the Devil as he does, and you can fill a church any day! What I want to know is how a man like that can bring himself to take four hundred a year out of the Church, when he doesn't believe one of the Articles he has sworn to?" Now the special offence of the liberal preacher on this occasion was a hint conveyed in a sermon that the fourth commandment in its entirety is hardly compatible with the life of an Englishman in the nineteenth century. And the laymen around are astounded by the man, feeling a great interest in him, not unmixed with awe. Has he come to them from Heaven or from Hell? Are these new teachings, which are not without their comfort, promptings direct from the Evil One, who is ever roaring for their souls, and who may thus have come to roar in their own parish? There is mystery as well as danger in the matter; and as mystery, and danger also when not too near, are both pleasant, the new man is not altogether unwelcome, in spite of the anathemas of the neighbouring rector. What if the new teaching should be true? So the men begin to speculate, and the women quake, and the neighbouring parsons are full of wrath, and the bishop's table groans with letters which he knows not how to answer, or how to leave unanswered. The free-thinking clergyman of whom we are speaking still creates much of this excitement in the country; but in the town he is encountered on easier terms, and in London he finds his own set, and has no special weight beyond that which his talents and his energy can give him.

It is very hard to come at the actual belief of any man. Indeed how should we hope to do so when we find it so very hard to come at our own? How many are there among us who, in this matter of our religion, which of all things is the most important to us, could take pen in hand and write down even for their own information exactly what they themselves believe? Not very many clergymen even, if so pressed, would insert boldly and plainly the fulminating clause of the Athanasian Creed; and yet each clergyman declares aloud that he believes it a dozen times every year of his life. Most men who call themselves Christians would say that they believed

the Bible, not knowing what they meant, never
having attempted,—and very wisely having refrained
from attempting amidst the multiplicity of their
worldly concerns,—to separate historical record from
inspired teaching. But when a liberal-minded clergyman does come among us,—come among us, that is,
as our pastor,—we feel not unnaturally a desire to
know what it is, at any rate, that he disbelieves. On
what is he unsound, according to the orthodoxy of
our old friend the neighbouring rector ? And are we
prepared to be unsound with him ? We know that
there are some things which we do not like in the
teaching to which we have been hitherto subjected ;—
that fulminating clause, for instance, which tells us
that nobody can be saved unless he believes a great
deal which we find it impossible to understand ; the
ceremonial Sabbath which we know that we do not
observe, though we go on professing that its observ-
ance is a thing necessary for us ;—the incompatibility
of the teaching of Old Testament records with the
new teachings of the rocks and stones. Is it within
our power to get over our difficulties by squaring our
belief with that of this new parson whom we acknow-

ledge at any rate to be a clever fellow ? Before we can do so we must at any rate know what is the belief,—or the unbelief,—that he has in him.

But this is exactly what we never can do. The old rector was ready enough with his belief. There were the three creeds, and the thirty-nine articles ; and, above all, there was the Bible,—to be taken entire, unmutilated, and unquestioned. His task was easy enough, and he believed that he believed what he said that he believed. But the new parson has by no means so glib an answer ready to such a question. He is not ready with his answer because he is ever thinking of it. The other man was ready because he did not think. Our new friend, however, is debonair and pleasant to us, with something of a subrisive smile in which we rather feel than know that there is a touch of irony latent. The question asked troubles him inwardly, but he is well aware that he should show no outward trouble. So he is debonair and kind,—still with that subrisive smile,— and bids us say our prayers, and love our God, and trust our Saviour. The advice is good, but still we want to know whether we are to pray God to help us to keep the Fourth Commandment, or only pretend so to pray,—and whether, when the fulminating clause is used, we are to try to believe it or to disbelieve it. We can only observe our new rector, and find out from his words and his acts how his own mind works on these subjects.

It is soon manifest to us that he has accepted the teaching of the rocks and stones, and that we may give up the actual six days, and give up also the deluge as a drowning of all the world. Indeed, we had almost come to fancy that even the old rector had become hazy on these points. And gradually there leak out to us, as to the falling of manna from heaven, and as to the position of Jonah within the whale, and as to the speaking of Balaam's ass, certain doubts, not expressed indeed, but which are made manifest to us as existing by the absence of expressions of belief. In the intercourse of social life we see something of a smile cross our new friend's face when the thirty-nine articles are brought down beneath his nose. Then he has read the *Essays and Reviews*, and will not declare his opinion that the writers of them should be unfrocked and sent away into chaos;—nay, we find that he is on terms of personal intimacy with one at least among the number of those writers. And, lastly, there comes out a subscription list for Bishop Colenso, and we find our new rector's name down for a five-pound note! That we regard as the sign, to be recognized by us as the most certain of all signs, that he has cut the rope which bound his barque to the old shore, and that he is going out to sea in quest of a better land. Shall we go with him, or shall we stay where we are?

If one could stay, if one could only have a choice in the matter, if one could really believe that the old shore is best, who would leave it? Who would not wish to be secure if he knew where security lay? But this new teacher, who has come among us with his ill-defined doctrines and his subrisive smile,—he and they who have taught him,—have made it impossible for us to stay. With hands outstretched towards the old places, with sorrowing hearts,—with hearts which still love the old teachings which the mind will no longer accept,—we, too, cut our ropes, and go out in our little boats, and search for a land that will be new to us, though how far new,—new in how

The Clergyman who Subscribes for Colenso

many things, we do not know. Who would not stay
behind if it were possible to him ?

But our business at present is with the teacher,
and not with the taught. Of him we may declare
that he is, almost always, a true man,—true in spite
of that subrisive smile and ill-defined doctrine. He
is one who, without believing, cannot bring himself
to think that he believes, or to say that he believes
that which he disbelieves without grievous suffering
to himself. He has to say it, and does suffer. There
are the formulas which must be repeated, or he must
abandon his ministry altogether,—his ministry, and
his adopted work, and the public utility which it is
his ambition to achieve. Debonair though he be,
and smile though he may, he has through it all some
terrible heart-struggles, in which he is often tempted
to give way and to acknowledge that he is too weak
for the work he has taken in hand. When he resolved
that he must give that five pounds to the Colenso
fund,—or rather when he resolved that he must have
his name printed in the public list, for an anonymous
giving of his money would have been nothing,—he
knew that his rope was indeed cut, and that his boat

was in truth upon the wide waters. After that it will serve him little to say that such an act on his part implies no agreement with the teaching of the African bishop. He had, by the subscription, attached himself to the Broad Church with the newest broad principles, and must expect henceforth to be regarded as little better than an infidel,—certainly as an enemy in the camp, — by the majority of his brethren of the day. "Why does he not give up his tithes? Why does he stick to his temporalities?" says the old-fashioned, wrathful parson of the neighbouring parish; and the sneer, which is repeated from day to day and from month to month, is not slow to reach the new man's ear. It is an accusation hard to be borne; but it has to be borne,—among other things,—by the clergyman who subscribes for Colenso.

THE END.